"Lloyd Rediger is not an outsider involved in clergy bashing or uncovering yet another reason to criticize the church. He is one of us, and he cares about the church, both its clergy and the community they are called to serve.... Rediger offers a strategy and some specific guidelines that emphasize responsible action to assist the church in supporting those in trouble."

Major General Stuart E. Barstad
(Retired) Chaplain, U.S. Air Force

"Wise counsel on a topic of increasing concern to the church and ministry. The richness of Rediger's experience in ministry to clergy is evident in this book."

John Patton, Professor of Pastoral Theology
Columbia Theological Seminary

"Dr. Rediger examines the critical dynamics that arise when religious leaders confront sexual ethics and the inevitable pain that ensues when ethics are compromised. Many facets of sexuality and spirituality are examined, and measures to prevent clergy misconduct are suggested. This is an important book on a vital topic facing contemporary religion."

Lloyd G. Sinclair, Midwest Center
for Sex Therapy, Madison, Wisconsin

"Dr. Rediger has opened for frank and candid discussion the whole area of clergy sexuality and its attendant consequences. The church needs to address these issues in an open and helpful way, and this book is the beginning of that journey— a journey that all Christians must share."

The Rt. Rev. Roger J. White
Episcopal Bishop of Milwaukee

"Sexual practices of clergy differ little from other persons. Dr. Rediger has clearly opened the case for informed discussion of clergy sexual issues. His candid, empathic, and astutely informed understanding of ministers, priests, and rabbis brings from the hush of whispered gossip to informed public discussion the sexual strengths and vulnerabilities of religious professionals. This is a daring venture to underscore public trust by open and frank discussion of lives that have been hurt by sexual problems. This is a helpful book because it points to ways for preventative as well as curative action for troubled clergy."

James W. Ewing, Director of Pastoral Care and
Counseling, United States International University

"Lloyd Rediger is informed, sympathetic, and above all, honest to clergy and their families. Reading the book made me hope that clergy and the churches would learn from his professional experiences a similar honesty and caring love. An important book for clergy, their families, and church leaders."

Denham Grierson, Executive Secretary
Victorian Council of Christian Education, Australia

CASES • COUNSELING • CARE

MINISTRY & SEXUALITY

G. Lloyd Rediger

FORTRESS PRESS   MINNEAPOLIS

MINISTRY AND SEXUALITY
Cases, Counseling, and Care

Scripture quotations unless otherwise noted are from the Revised Standard Version of the Bible, copyright © 1946, 1952, and 1971 by the Division of Christian Education of the National Council of Churches.

Cover design: Patty Paulus
Interior design: Publishers' WorkGroup

Library of Congress Cataloging-in-Publication Data

Rediger, G. Lloyd.
  Ministry and sexuality : cases, counseling, and care / G. Lloyd
Rediger.
      p.   cm.
  Includes bibliographical references.
  ISBN 0–8006–2418–1 (alk. paper)
  1. Clergy—Sexual behavior.   I. Title.
BV4392.R43   1990
253'.2—dc20   90–33422
                                                                  CIP

The paper used in this publication meets the minimum requirements of American National Standard for Information Sciences—Permanence of Paper for Printed Library Materials, ANSI Z329.48-1984. ∞™

Manufactured in the U.S.A.   AF 1–2418

94   93   92   91   90   1   2   3   4   5   6   7   8   9   10

To Shirley Grace Rediger

my beloved marriage partner
of thirty-eight years

CONTENTS

PART THREE
CASES IN OTHER CLERGY SEXUAL ISSUES

PART FOUR
CARE FOR CLERGY SEXUALITY

FOREWORD

Our society has experienced significant changes in sexual under-standings and behaviors in the past quarter century: in attitudes about homosexuality, in the practice of sexual expression out-side marriage, in the more open discussion of sexual matters, in the growing acceptance of new family forms. The changes have come not only in society at large but also in religious reinter-pretations. Like every other major shift in human perceptions and behaviors, these sexual changes are marked by ambiguity in the culture and in the church. Never before in Christian history has there been so much open discussion of sexuality issues, so many task force reports, so many denominational pronounce-ments, so many church groups organized to press further change or to reverse it, so many heated debates, and so much church pain and division around sexuality matters.

In spite of all the ambiguities, many of us celebrate much that is happening. We celebrate the fundamental challenges to those ancient dualisms that split spirit from body, thought from feel-ing, and men from women. We embrace the cultural movement toward more wholistic and egalitarian understandings of the person, remarkably akin to the vision at the core of biblical reve-lation. We join in the quest to reunite sexuality and spirituality, a union essential to an incarnational faith. We affirm the current reassessment of sexual moralities and moralisms, seeking a gospel ethic that is nonlegalistic but centered in responsibility and integrity. We join in acknowledging that the church is a sexual community with sexual understandings informing its theologies, pieties, worship, education, leadership patterns, and social witness—sexual understandings that frequently need serious reexamination. We profit from the fresh insights into the pervasive ways that sexuality, always a deeply personal issue, is also inescapably a public issue affecting our responses to every form of social oppression and every opportunity for greater justice. Such are some of the remarkable gains of the sexual reassessment in recent years.

But the gains themselves are incomplete, often spotty. The church still has considerable difficulty in dealing creatively and forthrightly with sexuality. The destructive sexual dualisms, while freshly acknowledged, have not vanished. Anxieties, fears, and uncertainties almost paralyze us in many ways. We are often more reactive than proactive. We are unclear about the sources for our sexual theologies and about the patterns of life that should flow from them. In so many ways the church is "an uncertain trumpet" when it comes to providing sexual leadership.

The sexual problems experienced by clergy are one important element in this uncertainty. Long a subject skittishly approached and surreptitiously dealt with, it is now a matter demanding forthright address. Whether there actually are more sexual problems among clergy now than in earlier times is difficult to say, but several things are clear. It is evident that many clergy are confused by the transitional times that are upon us. Further, we are considerably more aware of the clergy problems that do exist, for they now receive more attention from ecclesiastical officers, elicit more coverage—sometimes sensational—by the media, and end up more often in the courtroom. Fortunately, we now have better tools for understanding the dynamics of many sexual problems and the therapeutic resources with which to address them.

The images, expectations, and roles of clergy, however, make the subject still difficult to broach frankly and constructively. Dr. Rediger's eminently useful, insightful, and courageous book grasps that nettle boldly, and I count it a privilege to introduce it. With many years as a professional counselor of clergy, he is remarkably equipped for the task. He understands deeply the life, the dynamics, the stresses, and the possibilities of professional ministry. His compassion, his own ethical integrity, and his deep concern for clergy and for the church are all imprinted on these pages.

I am struck by many features of this book. Dr. Rediger is frank without sacrificing sensitivity. His premise, which I endorse, is that it is valuable to the health of both clergy and the church to be specific about these sexual problems. In his forthright approach, he embodies the pastoral guidelines that he recommends to others: nonjudgmental acceptance, careful listening, a caring response to pain, the development and pursuit of a strategy, and assistance in turning a difficult experience into an opportunity for change and growth. Indeed, one of the book's values is the reader's opportunity to observe a skillful counselor in action as he deals with actual cases from his experience.

I celebrate Dr. Rediger's strong affirmation both of clergy and of God's gift of human sexuality. At the beginning of the book he expresses concern that his focus on problems might suggest a negative tone about our present church leadership. This is not his intent. He knows clergy from the inside (himself included), honors the difficult and sacred trust of the office, and rejoices in the sexual health of the majority. Nor is it his intent to present sexuality as a particularly fallen or suspect dimension of our humanity. He advocates a positive sensuous spirituality and acknowledges the sexual bases for human intimacy of all kinds. These features deserve underscoring when a book by design gives major attention to the problematics in both ministers and sex. Further, the author is clear about his own norms regarding intimacy and sexual expression. Yet he refrains from claiming finality for his own ethical understandings and presents his norms in ways that do not oversimplify complex life situations.

A book such as this cannot be utterly inclusive, nor does the author purport to be. Yet the range of issues he tackles is astounding. In limited space Dr. Rediger gives an impressive amount of attention not only to the problematics of certain sexual expressions but also to some of their underlying dynamics. Of particular importance, he attends to prevention as well as treatment. In medical terms, he is concerned not only with disease cure but at least as much with health care.

One area that we all need to work at understanding these days is the dynamics of *male* sexuality in both its distortions and its health. The majority of Dr. Rediger's problem cases have male subjects. This is surely understandable; there are still many more male than female clergy. But it is also striking that so many of the problems herein treated stem from an excessive genitalization of sexual feelings and meanings, a pattern much more typical of men's sexual experience than women's. In matters of counseling and therapy, but just as surely in basic issues of theology and spirituality, we need to give more attention to these gender matters. The male side of that attention is currently underdeveloped, precisely because our patriarchal heritage has led us to assume that it is normative.

There are points where I would differ with Dr. Rediger—and surely he with me—in accent and even, occasionally, in substance. These are far outweighed, however, by our agreements. One of those many agreements is so basic to both a psychology and a theology of sexuality that I wish to underscore it in conclusion. It is an understanding that I find implied throughout this fine book: The erotic dynamism of the human self does not aim primarily at sensual pleasure—as good as that is—but more basically and fundamentally at *communion*. That is God's design. Thus, when sexual expressions go awry and become harmful to others, to oneself, and to the ministry, our hunger for communion has not been replaced by something else. What has happened is that *eros*, the hunger and desire for connection, is, for the moment, being expressed destructively. What may appear as a mechanical, obsessive, alien instinct actually represents the

individual's desperate attempts to establish meaningful communion with the other, with the self, and with God. Both hopeful
counseling and creative sexual theology are grounded in that
recognition. I see that basic conviction on the pages that follow,
and that is one of the many reasons I find this book important.
I hope it will be widely read.

JAMES B. NELSON
United Theological Seminary
of the Twin Cities

PREFACE

This book about the rising incidence of clergy sexual problems is written with an ecumenical perspective and nineteen years of confidential data. The information was gathered at the Office of Pastoral Services (OPS) of the Wisconsin Conference of Churches, at which clergy from thirty denominations have been counseled over the years. Deep appreciation is due John Fischer, executive director of the Wisconsin Conference of Churches, and to my colleagues on that staff; to the ecumenically representative committee, faithful in oversight, that has governed OPS; and to the Reverend John R. Thomas and the visionary denominational executives who founded OPS during 1967 to 1970. For the past seventeen years, Jeanne Maruska, my administrative assistant at OPS, has provided extraordinary sensitivity, competence, and pastoral care in daily operations. She has been a valued partner in offering her perspective on the issues, as well as in editing and typing the manuscript.

I thank James B. Nelson, professor of Christian ethics at United Theological Seminary of the Twin Cities, who, as my seminary adviser and mentor and as a prophetic voice of Christian wisdom regarding human sexuality, has given valuable insights. Executives and friends in the church have surrounded me all of my life. They are not responsible for what I have written, but I thankfully acknowledge their dedication to Christian caring and support for my ministry. Finally, I thank the editors at Fortress Press who have seen the need for this book and have guided it to completion.

A subject as sensitive as the one treated in this book is likely to evoke strong feelings in readers. I feel some dismay at the negative view this book implies regarding leaders of the church. Perhaps this can be balanced by my expression of personal admiration for the vast majority of clergy I have known, and by my personal witness to the joy of ministry that I have experienced as a pastor and pastoral counselor since 1950. Even with its frustrations and pain, I know of no other calling that provides as much satisfaction and opportunity to be a nurturing and intimate partner with so many persons on their spiritual pilgrimage through life. I thank God and the church for the privilege of my call to be a pastor.

MINISTRY AND SEXUALITY

INTRODUCTION

Maybe there is a third sex—clergy. If this is true, it is the clergy role, not the clergyperson, that is that third sex. Indeed, it is this role, entrusted to vulnerable people, that can imply that clergy are not normal. In clergy sexual scandals not only is there sexual misconduct but there is also *malfeasance*—the violation of expectations and the breaking of public trust. Yet contemporary society still imagines that clergy are somehow different from other persons, that clergy do not have normal human appetites and needs, and that they are spiritually and morally superior to ordinary mortals. We know that this is untrue.

I seek by offering my own perspective and experience to address an honest church that will better clarify the clergy role in relation to congregations, that will better understand the humanness of clergy (their legitimate needs and extraordinary vulnerability), and that will establish better personal, congregational, peer, and denomination support systems. My purpose is to prompt the needed discussion by reporting on clergy sexual misconduct and by reflecting on other clergy sexual issues.

Sexual malfeasance by clergy is a distortion of spiritual leadership. When it occurs, the church has a responsibility to intervene, limit, prescribe healing, and determine readiness to resume the pastoral office. Malfeasant clergy have a responsibility to

confess, recover, and reorder their lives, to attend to the consequences of their behavior in the lives of others, and to work
toward the prevention of such malfeasance in their own lives
and those of their peers. The rising incidence of clergy moral
malfeasance requires that the church reexamine and reconstitute
systemic clergy support mechanisms. The moral health of the
clergy is crucial to the moral health of the church.

My research indicates that approximately 10 percent of clergy
(mostly male) have been or are engaged in sexual malfeasance.
Another 15 percent are on the verge—waiting for an opportunity. Many of these clergy do not realize how vulnerable and
close to disaster they are. Seventy-five percent of clergy are functioning well; but they, too, are more vulnerable than previous
generations, due to the inadequacy of the typical clergy support
process. One of the reasons for this book is to urge the church
and society to move beyond the titillating and recriminative
attention it gives to the notorious 10 percent of clergy and to
concentrate more helpful attention on the 15 percent and the 75
percent who have real or potential vulnerabilities.

BASIS OF BOOK

Each case study in Parts 2 and 3 is factual. Some specifics may
be generalized to make a broader point than a specific situation
allows. The case material is drawn from my many years of experience as a confidential counselor to clergy and their families,
many workshops and consultations I have led, frequent dialogue
with church leaders responsible for the care and oversight of
clergy, and extensive international travel.

The base population for the case studies in this book is the
clergy population of the midwestern United States—especially
Wisconsin, which is among the most heavily churched states in
the United States. This provides an intensive and focused perspective on the functioning of clergy. The clergy (and their families) who have consulted with me at the Office of Pastoral
Services are primarily mainline Protestant. Yet our case files

contain enough experience with fundamentalists and evangelicals, as well as Roman Catholic and Jewish religious leaders,
that I feel their unique perspectives are included here. I would
not claim, however, to speak authoritatively on any but mainline
Protestant clergy problems.

PLAN OF BOOK

The strategy of this book is to indicate the context and counseling of clergy sexual problems, present cases demonstrating problem areas or issues of clergy sexuality, and discuss prescriptive
possibilities. Part 1 elaborates my experience at the Office of
Pastoral Services in working with clergy who, voluntarily or by
mandate from judicatory officials, have sought assistance with
sexual problems or issues. This part presents my understanding
of human wholeness and sexuality, the star factor as lending
vulnerability to sexual malfeasance, and the need to view sexual
malfeasance from the perspective of the victim.

Part 2 organizes clergy sexual malfeasances by grouping them
in generic form under the rubric of addiction. I have learned
much from the addictive and codependency theories. Treatments
now developed for a variety of maladies can be used effectively
in the context of sexual addictions.

Part 3 gathers together other sexual issues. This is a sundry
list. These are important for the church's discussion of ministry
and sexuality. Yet they do not, in my opinion, fit under the rubric
of addiction. Nor, for that matter, do they form a whole.

Part 4 provides resources for managing and preventing clergy
sexual malfeasance. One chapter features some very specific
guidelines in clergy sexual ethics that emphasize responsible
action. Systemic prevention and support for clergy and their
families are discussed. The need for intimacy—which affects malfeasance and sexual issues—is detailed in the final chapter.

Throughout I use several terms that should be defined at the
outset. By *gender programming*, I mean the training and expectations given to boys and girls as they grow up. Gender program-

ming establishes gender roles by teaching girls what it means to be female and boys what it means to be male in a particular culture and time. By *gender revolution,* I am referring to the recent challenges to more traditional role stereotypes. As a result of this, men and women are freer to adopt roles that differ from the traditional stereotypes. By *sexual revolution,* I have in mind the changes of the last three decades that permit more open, homosexual, bisexual, and heterosexual liaisons than the traditional monogamous sexual union. I take the sexual revolution to be one factor in the larger gender revolution.

In this book, I am advocating that the church continue to develop an open and frank discussion of sexual malfeasances and sexual issues, that clergy take more conscious responsibility for managing their own lives, and that the church develop better systems of support for clergy and for congregations. The traditional forms of support, with few exceptions, are not adequate. We need to rethink the clergy role and support process in contemporary terms.

PART ONE

COUNSELING, CLERGY, AND VICTIMS

1

COUNSELING CLERGY WITH SEXUAL PROBLEMS

In the past twenty years, we in the church have witnessed a revolution in clergy sexual behavior overall and the incidence of sexual malfeasance by clergy in particular. In 1970, the clergy I counseled were typically male caucasians caught in conflicts in their congregations or denominations. About that time the surge in clergy divorces brought a demand for more marriage counseling. In the late seventies, women and single clergy (mostly male) presented a different variety of problems and needs. More recently there has been a significant increase in clergy sexual malfeasance (Part 2) and issues of sexual orientation and preference (Part 3). This pattern, a microcosm of the revolutionary changes in sexual practices and attitudes in society, seems to be the result of several causes: Clergy often want to break out of role stereotypes and be "like other people"; there is a breakdown of denominational patterns of discipline and support; clergy typically experience high stress and minimal support in their ministries.

The health of clergy and the church requires that we be open and specific about the sexual problems of clergy. Some leaders believe that the less said the better, but I have not found this to be true. The sexual problems of clergy with which I have worked multiply more from secrecy and privacy than from openness.

Secrecy tends to heighten fascination, addiction, guilt, fear, and begets an illusion that there will be no negative consequences; privacy tends to keep fantasies and opportunities for illicit liaisons from the influence of common sense and peer review.

Clergy sexual malfeasance and other issues are best handled through informed support in confidential and caring ways. I have neither easy answers nor quick cures. I have used and developed some perspectives and methods, however, that appear to be helpful. Furthermore, in naming and confronting clergy sexual problems and in openly discussing clergy sexual issues, we are finding opportunities to provide pastoring for those who have no pastor (that is, clergy and their families), to listen and to learn together about human sexuality, and to probe deeply into the spiritual resources of the church and its clergy. In the short term, we are trying to facilitate healing. In the long term, we are trying to understand causes and effects, revise theology and denominational policies, clarify professional ethics, and encourage better strategies for management, prevention, and spiritual growth.

We begin by openly acknowledging that clergypersons have genitalia. This is a fact of life. Men and women need to reflect on this fact to understand how different they are from each other and, at the same time, how much they are involved with each other in bodily complementarity, creative activity, and spiritual communion. Clergy men and women need to reflect on the givenness of their genitalia because this can break open the mystique of the sexual guilt that can be such a burdensome part of the clergy role. It can help clergy to understand that they are people, too. It can also heighten their sensitivity to human yearnings and spiritual experience because appropriate sexual experience is a metaphor for the highest spiritual experience—union with God, creation, and each other.

We also need to recognize that sexuality and spirituality are intertwined. When blended, they augment and inform each other. James Nelson in his work on human sexuality has been prophetic in exploring and describing the nurturing union of sexuality and spirituality. Not only does he discuss the fallacies connected with sex and spirituality, he celebrates their union. His constant emphasis is on body—the human, physical body—because our understanding and experience have this as the primary reference. Sexuality, for example, is not something we do with our bodies, it is an expression of our bodies. Spirituality, then, is not the transcendence of our bodies but the celebration of our body-selves.

COUNSELING COMMITMENTS

As a credentialed pastoral counselor for the church, I function in some ways as an authority figure. When it is appropriate, therefore, I may share my sexual experiences and beliefs. But my primary task is to offer acceptance of the person, with the promise of understanding. As the clergyperson and I try to understand her or his predicament, this person will see more clearly the important issues. My own work with clergy in sexual dilemmas has been guided by five general commitments that I think are the basis of all pastoral counseling.

First, when clergy are in sexual trouble or anxious to explore sexual issues, they need nonjudgmental acceptance, not because nothing is wrong, but because without unconditional acceptance, the clergyperson is tied in emotional and rational knots. Make the exploration of sexual issues as free as possible of judgmental strictures.

Second, the counselor needs to listen carefully to hear what this person sees as the problem or opportunity, and what he or she wants to do about it. The presented problem may not be the real issue, and what the counselee first claims to be a necessary course of action may not be what is actually wanted or what would be most effective. Active listening, as it is often called, begins with listening but continues with reflective response and probing inquiry.

Third, whatever the problem, the counselor needs to respond caringly to pain. This means allowing ample time for the pain to be expressed, and then acknowledging it in a sensitive way. The task can be complicated when dealing with a couple or family in which one of the participants has brought pain to another participant; but when the pain is drawn out and evidence of caring is offered, perpetrators can understand some of the consequences of their behavior and benefit from the counseling process.

Fourth, the counselor needs to enable the clergyperson to develop and pursue a strategy that has the promise of being effective. The most successful solutions are those motivated by a person's own decisions, and most healthy persons want to be in charge of their own lives; but sometimes they need to be reminded that they can be. They also need to be reminded that being in charge means dealing with consequences of their behavior.

Finally, the counselor needs to assist the counselee in turning the experience into a change and growth opportunity. This actually occurs throughout the process as issues are identified, pain eased, and strategy and action developed. It is as important for clergy as for anyone else to put new insights into practice. Such changes require a supportive environment.

WHOLENESS AS A THEOLOGICAL ANCHOR

The root meaning of the word "wholeness" in Scripture is salvation, peace. I use several facets of biblical wholeness to undergird and guide my own counseling.

Biblical wholeness does not always parallel human thoughts and feelings. We seek our own comfort and associate with those who share our biases. But our comfort and like-minded friends can be at odds with God's purposes in creation. Part of that creation is our sex organs, our sexual urges and appetites, our sexual identity, and our sexual activity. God's purpose is not that we satisfy our sexual urges only but that we also discipline our sexual expressions. Biblical wholeness has to do with how we embody our sexual identity.

Wholeness is inclusive; it has polarities and is not static.

Rhythms and cycles such as work and rest, night and day, joy and sorrow, being and doing need to be blended. Thus, seeking a magical state of bliss is less than wholistic. Our sexual identity is more than a pleasurable orgasm. It includes both pleasure and continence.

Biblical wholeness includes the total human being—body, mind, and spirit. Separating genital pleasure from emotional, intellectual, and spiritual well-being distorts the ability of each to enrich and be enriched by the other aspects. Furthermore, wholeness includes others—whether or not they are present. Our sexual acts, expressions of sexual identity, or embodiment include disagreement, discomfort, and frustration.

Finally, wholeness requires communication within ourselves, between us and other persons, and between persons and God. This yields internal clarification. It allows us to understand, have fellowship, and negotiate among persons. It also allows interaction between humans and that which is greater than their community: God and creation. Beliefs, standards, and values are reinforced through such communication and are reflected in our sexuality.

ROLE-SPECIFIC STRATEGIES

In addition to these counseling commitments and theological anchors for counseling, my own experience and reflection indicates that eight role-specific strategies are also important when counseling clergy or their families.

First, be practical. What works in the office may not work back home. Clergy, like everyone, are part of a system or systems. The one-to-one, couple, or family strategies need to be adapted when denominational executives, lay leaders, and significant peers are in action. Some therapies try to assemble all involved parties so that every aspect of the issue is explored and all persons become responsible for resolution. The congregations or power groups usually associated with clergy sexual problems, however, are unwieldy. Usually I invite the counselee to imagine or chart the responses back home. Sometimes I have gone to the church setting and met with involved parties in small groups or congregational meetings, using sermons, workshops, and group exercises to facilitate strategies.

Second, check the accuracy of the clergyperson's understanding of denominational policy, theological anchors, and personal faith regarding this matter. There are so many moral oughts and shoulds built into our perceptions that clarifying becomes important. Otherwise, the counselor and clergyperson miscommunicate—each imagining that the other understands reality in the same way.

Third, be direct. It is easy to take counseling style cues from the clergyperson or spouse, to be overly cautious and overly nice, especially when dealing with sexual matters. We clergy have a way of seducing others into being nice. This works against us when trying to deal with tough issues. But I have found that even nice clergy appreciate a counselor who will cut through the euphemisms and game-playing to identify the key issues. This is an endorsement not for nastiness, but for confronting the real issues.

Fourth, promptly address any impediment the counselor's gender may pose. The gender of the counselor may or may not be an obstruction. Clergy of both sexes now seem to have little trouble discussing sexual issues with pastoral counselors of either gender, as long as they believe the counselor to be competent and trustworthy. But homosexual clergy, for example, seem to be more wary of male pastoral counselors. This seems quite normal, since male clergy have often been their primary oppressors. Once the issue is open for discussion, it can be dealt with much like any other sexual issue.

Fifth, explore and state the limits of absolute confidentiality. There are usually three limits: legal action (almost any records and testimony can be subpoenaed by the courts when a fee is paid for the counseling); abuse (when abuse and injury has occurred or is likely to occur); and incompetency (when the counselee is unable to manage himself or herself adequately and engages in behavior inappropriate to the clergy role). This can be an exceedingly complicated issue. On one hand, confidentiality has been used by clergy and the church to conceal sexual malfeasance. On the other hand, clergy deserve and need confidential help as they work out some sexual problems. Clergy reputations are extraordinarily sensitive to sexual scandal. Therefore, if confidentiality is to be broken, the counselor must be certain of the facts and be ready to handle the consequences.

Sixth, relate the issues to religious faith. Clergy often need to be reminded of the resources of their personal faith and training. They who minister grace to others may forget that grace applies to them also.

Seventh, be prepared to deal with basic data and information. Not all clergy are well informed or experienced in understanding the fundamentals of human sexuality.

Eighth, maintain and nurture your own intimacy. It is not unusual for counselors to come to sexual counseling situations in a personally vulnerable state. Because clergy are expected to be highly visible moral role models, the counselor whose intimate vulnerability is poorly managed may also transfer such expectations or vulnerable needs onto the clergyperson. Neither projection is responsible counseling.

Human beings manage their lives by means of a self-concept and images of success or relational priorities. These are formulated early in life and modified with experience. The goals and expectations of a person's peers, elders, and society in general not only offer the raw materials for the individual's mental images of self and success or relational priorities, they also give feedback about how well the individual is doing in the society. Responsible counseling elicits and examines these mental images and feedbacks.

Each child grows up in a setting that offers a general view of human beings and the good life. Three models tend to shape our society's views: the American dream, which suggests freedom and happiness as the key to life; the medical model, which suggests that getting rid of illness and disabilities is the key; and the psychological model, which suggests the absence of hang-ups as the key. All of these are valuable, but they leave out the fact that human beings are a combination of physical, emotional, and spiritual factors. Focusing attention on one factor often leaves the other two crippled in some way; people need a vision of human wholeness. Responsible counseling seeks to articulate and explore each person's vision of human wholeness.

2

THE STAR FACTOR

Clergy do not typically think of themselves as stars. In fact, one of the expectations of the clergy role is humility, even self-effacement. These expectations, however, do not prevent clergy stardom; they in fact breed a stereotypical modesty that fulfills others' expectations while leaving unfulfilled the need for stardom—the desire to be recognized as the leader.

The term star describes the unique combination of being the identified spiritual leader of a congregation, a recognizable moral leader in the community, and a performer in the spotlight leading people in their liturgical worship of God. This is heady—even in an increasingly secularized society. No other profession offers an individual the responsibility of standing in front of an audience at least once every week and interpreting God, life, and morality for them. No amount of humility, denial, or self-effacement can alter the immense stimulation and satisfaction derived from this regular opportunity.

THE STAR FACTOR AND SEXUALITY

The clergy role is not intended to be sexy, but it is closely connected to the lure of human sexuality for several reasons. There is a normal human person inside the role, with all the usual human needs and appetites. The role carries with it the natural charisma of mystical closeness to God. This mystique is intriguing for both the possessor and the observer. There is a real or implied power attached to this role—power to judge, reward, advise, and scandalize. The addition of physical attractiveness and pleasant style can generate a sexual aura that captivates, inspires, and deludes.

Then there is clerical orgasm—the performance of the liturgy and the delivery of the sermon. No wonder clergy often feel euphoric during and then exhausted after public worship. No wonder the audience—the faithful—feel attracted, fascinated, inspired, and sometimes disappointed, for the event of public worship can reach into the innermost self, the source of energy, stimulation, and satisfaction.

This description of clergy functioning is not intended to be cynical or sacrilegious. Rather, it is intended as a reminder of the deep relationship between spirituality and sexuality, as a warning about the volatility of the clergy role, and as a description of what I have seen in confidential counseling and seminars. I find a consistent connection between the stimulation of the role and the attraction and satisfaction derived from role performance. We typically think of all this in terms of moral and spiritual leadership. Indeed, it is. But from my experience we can no longer ignore the sexual dimensions of the role. Further, we must prepare clergy, clergy spouses, and parishioners to understand this process, lest we be trapped by it.

The clergy role has always been sexually stimulating. It was usually controlled, however, by tradition, training, spiritual disciplines, intimate support systems, and fear. These controls have all been somewhat eroded in recent generations. In this past generation the sexual revolution, clergy divorces, constant sexual stimulation from the media, the glamorizing of celebrities such as televangelists, the heightened intensity of life, the loss of family controls, and the breakdown of denominational disciplines have produced a volatile experience that tends to loosen restrictions around genital expression.

DYNAMICS OF THE STAR FACTOR

The star factor is attractive, especially from a masculine perspective. Having people gather at least once a week to listen to what you have to say is a real high. Even though leading public worship and preaching are not always easy, comfortable, or applauded, there is a fascination and stimulation that comes with being the leader of an organization. The star factor also includes power—to make things happen, to affect people's lives, to control policy, and to generate more and more power and influence. Power has long been an aphrodisiac, in both its legitimate and illegitimate forms. Clergy do not often have or exercise raw power, but their role provides significant opportunities for influence and control.

One of the subtlest and most significant ingredients in the star factor is the self-concept that develops when the clergy role is internalized. A pastor may begin to believe that he is an unusually capable and privileged person, to imagine that moral rules and principles do not apply to him because he is above responsibility, or that shortcuts and exceptions are acceptable in his case. Then theology can incorporate the belief that because he is called of God and doing such noble work, he can make his own rules.

The star factor makes some people imagine that they are released from human limitations and responsibilities. A star does not need to pay attention to physical, emotional, and spiritual health, for these apply only to ordinary people. The star must be free to perform—to do whatever needs to be done to be outstanding. Such thinking leads to professional and personal burnout and is a distortion of spiritual leadership.

For the star factor to operate, there needs to be a performer and appreciative observers. Human beings seem to need heroes. Some need to be heroes. In the unspoken contract between performer and audience, each gets something it wants. The performer gets an audience, and the audience gets a performer. But there are price tags on such transactions. The performer must keep doing whatever wins applause, and the audience limits its role to that of observation, with little satisfaction from participation.

The star factor contributes significantly to clergy sexual malfeasance by blinding the performer and the admiring observer to the realities of meaningful, responsible relationships. Each may confuse the attraction for the other as true love, and act out the sexual dimension of love without making either the investments in each other or the commitment to responsible relationships that happiness and ministry require. Being a star is essentially a lonely life. The star may be surrounded by groupies and followers but dares not reveal human characteristics that may disillusion the audience. Therefore, basic human needs are not met, and authenticity is sacrificed. The audience does not really care for the performer, and the performer loses real contact with the audience.

RESPONSIBILITY FOR THE SITUATION

The dynamics of the star factor are common knowledge. What does not seem to be common is the recognition that heightened sexual stimulation and the relaxing of controls, combined with the clergy's opportunities for privacy and intimate contact, will inevitably produce the significant increase in sexual malpractice and scandalous affairs that we now see in clergy circles. Responsibility for the current situation must be shared by all.

Clergy Responsibility

Clergy, it must be emphasized, bear primary responsibility for their own sexual conduct, and consciousness-raising is needed to enable clergy to be alert to the sexual pitfalls of their role. Some still seem to think sexual malfeasance happens only to other clergy, not to themselves.

My research at OPS shows two typical patterns in the lives of clergy with sexual problems. One pattern shows persons who have never resolved primary sexual issues in their lives and have a long history of poor sexual self-management. The other pattern indicates persons who allow their primary intimate relationship, usually marriage, to deteriorate until it is no longer supportive. This pattern also typically includes a life-style of poor stress management and loss of spiritual commitment and discipline. In this way, the star is born.

I have also found that most clergy do not receive clear instruction in their denomination's moral ethics policies and are not given enough guidance and support in how to manage their personal lives so that sexual issues can be handled well. An annual clergy checkup is needed to provide pastors, priests, and rabbis with an opportunity to review their management of their personal and professional lives. This helps them to regain a healthy perspective if they have lost it and to develop realistic goals and strategies for self-fulfillment and faithfulness in ministry.

Congregational Responsibility

Parishioners also need to share some of the responsibility for the sexual malfeasance of clergy. Parishioners typically do not understand the shared nature of pastoral ministry. It is common for them to think that they "pay the pastor to do the work of the church," and that they carry little responsibility for the congregation's ministry. In fact, they often think the pastor exists to please them. Traditional volunteer services in the church and old-fashioned concern for the pastor are eroding. This results in pastors feeling more and more alone, resenting the unrealistic work expectations, and therefore becoming vulnerable to using sex inappropriately as a coping mechanism.

In such a situation, people are not aware of danger signals. It is obvious in most cases of sexual malfeasance by clergy that the congregation was not aware of problems until too late and did not provide adequate support and accountability for the pastor. Then when sexual problems occur, they tend to feel that their star has betrayed them and to become angry, critical, and vindictive toward the fallen pastor. Fortunately, in most situations there are parishioners and peers who find ways to care for the pastor, even though professional ethics have been violated. But, in too many cases there is a heavy toll of hurt and ill will.

Denominational Responsibility

Most denominational executives do a conscientious job of dealing with sexual malfeasance among their clergy. This does not mean that they do what needs to be done. Most denominational executives, it is true, are overworked, have few resources for oversight unless clergy are sources of trouble, have inadequate training for spotting early warning signs, and must overreact when confronted with malfeasance in order to respond to the outrage of laity. But denominational executives are also responsible. They worry about the massive disruption that occurs in a denomination when sexual malfeasance is discovered and dealt with openly. More than this, some bishops and executives are involved in sexual irregularities themselves. Therefore, there is a tendency by some denominational executives to avoid, deny, and even cover sexual malfeasance. Most skirt or avoid altogether other sexual issues.

It is very difficult to deal with clergy sexual malfeasance under public scrutiny. The sense of outrage, betrayal, mistrust, and threat is capable of overwhelming the gentler emotions and reactions, such as compassion, forgiveness, humility, and good judgment. So a normal first reaction from a denominational executive upon discovering a clergyperson's sexual malfeasance is to avoid it or try to deal with it privately, punishing in ways that do not draw public attention to this issue. How does anyone compassionately decide a course of action between ending and punishing clergy sexual abuse of a young boy, for example, and compassion and healing for the clergyperson involved? How does anyone wisely adjudicate between a congregation accusing a pastor of having an affair and the pastor who denies the accusation? How does a denominational executive decide appropriate punishment or recovery requirements for two pastors when one is a close personal friend or power broker and the other pastor is not? How does a denominational executive deal with a sexual issue regarded as sin by some constituents and as acceptable by others? When the tenure of most denominational executives is determined politically, we can expect the answers to such questions to be decided by political factors. From my perspective, this is less than responsible.

This chapter may appear to be an overstatement of the realities of pastoral leadership and sexual malfeasance by clergy. Most are faithful ministers with the integrity we have come to expect; only a small proportion succumb to the pitfalls possible when living the clergy role in contemporary society. It is to their victims that we now turn.

3

SEXUAL VICTIMS

It is nearly impossible for anyone who has not been victimized sexually to comprehend the enormity of the experience. The feelings of victims explode. They speak of terror, violation, helplessness, betrayal, anguish, shame, and rage; they scream or whisper, look at you with haunted eyes, curl up in the fetal position—unless they have been through therapy or have buried the experience within themselves long ago. We do not know how to handle all this well, either in our society or in the church. So many victims have survived and appear to be relatively normal that we do not notice the long-term effects of their devastation. In fact, victims often are unaware of the deep effects within themselves, until someone assists in uncovering and resolving them.

STATISTICS

Statistics on sexual issues are difficult to gather, assess, and interpret. Researchers are hard-pressed to provide terms, measurements, and settings for gathering reliable data. Terminology, questions, and motivations are subject to the idiosyncrasies of personal experience and are influenced by media and peer perspectives. The base populations from which the data are gathered may not be typical of the general population. (This is certainly true of my own counseling; the clergy are either self-selected or sent to me by judicatory executives.) The interpretation of the data and experiences also is not standardized. Therefore, statistics on sexual abuse mean different things to different people. Some general data, nevertheless, seem established.

1. The majority of sexual offenders seek out more than one victim.
2. The majority of offenders are involved in more than one type of sexual offense.
3. Patterns that sometimes later result in sexual offenses typically begin at an early age.
4. Sexual offenses are seldom random or accidental. The acts are typically the result of long-term masturbatory fantasies and inappropriate sexual self-management.
5. There is sometimes a pattern of violence and certainly abusive behavior attendant to sexual offenses. Verbal harassment and physical abuse are common. These can be subtle and manipulative, as well as overt.
6. Some offenders have a pattern of progressive movement toward overt offenses. Less frequently the pattern shows constant belligerence and violence toward society and victims.
7. Low self-esteem and insecurity are characteristics of sexual offenders.
8. There are several levels of victims of sexual offenses: first and foremost, the person suffering the immediate offense; second, victims such as family, spouse, peer groups, and society; and finally, the offender.
9. Bisexuals and heterosexuals are significantly more likely to commit sexual abuse on children than homosexuals, based upon their percentages in the population.
10. Nearly all victims of sexual abuse by professionals report experiences of shock, suppression of the memory, guilt about their own falsely presumed responsibility, and worry that no one would believe their report of abuse.
11. Treatment patterns for offenders and victims are presently

helping to express care and provide some limits. They are not yet statistically effective, for there is significant repetition of violation of many victims and high recidivism rates for perpetrators.

12. A much smaller percentage of tax dollars is spent on treatment than on prosecution.

Following are representative and competent statistics to assist us in understanding the victimization occurring in sexual offenses in the United States and the church.

1. Approximately 27 percent of women and 16 percent of men in the United States have been sexually and physically abused.
2. Approximately 25 percent of sexual offenders were abused as children.
3. A small percentage of all sex offenders commits the vast majority of sex crimes. These are the hard-core offenders.
4. Clergy sex offenders follow patterns similar to those of the general population.
5. Less than 2 percent of victims of sexual offenses receive competent professional therapy.

VICTIM AND OFFENDER CHARACTERISTICS

There is no dependable profile of characteristics by which either victim or offender can be identified by outside observation. However, the self-reports and data from therapists do show factors worth noting.

Victims

Victims are usually female, young, and surprised. They are often targeted by the offender without their knowledge. They may be alone, in a group, on a date or family outing. They may be sexually experienced or virgins. They may be seductive, consciously or unconsciously. They may tease and challenge. But nothing erases the fact that they are victims.

When the victims are boys, or occasionally men, the circumstances may be as seemingly random as for girls and women.
But they, too, have often been targeted in the fantasies of the
offender. Boys are even less wary than girls of abusive sex, for
they are often not taught that their bodies are sexually attractive
to certain other human beings. Also, boys are typically more
curious and experimental with sex. This makes them more vulnerable to men (and occasionally women) who entice them with
playfulness or rewards. Boys can be streetwise and seductive
and even collude naively or intentionally, to some degree, in
their own victimization. But none of this changes the fact that
they are victims.

Fortunately, the courts are less inclined to view victims as responsible for their victimization. It is more common now for
courts to emphasize the rights of victims and to determine the
trial process from the victim's perspective. Victims need every
consideration.

Offenders

Offenders come in all sizes, ages, and racial and cultural back-
grounds. There is no single profile that identifies the sex offender.
But some general characteristics are apparent to careful observation. Boys or men who are sex offenders often come from homes
they describe as troubled, where love and healthy self-management were not modeled. They most typically are fascinated by
sex. This attraction begins at an early age. In school, they may
well have been known for their sexual acting out. Also typically,
they learned to connect self-gratification with sex objects, that is,
they fantasized sex acts with anonymous or known sex partners
while masturbating. Pornography in some form is often a factor.
This combination often identifies the hard-core sex offender.

Other addictions are commonly associated with the addiction
to sex. Substance abuse, overeating, and many pleasurable
activities can be combined. This kind of sexuality is marked by
its compulsiveness, its imaginative modes, and its being out of

control much of the time, whether or not this is known to the offender and associates. Any control is usually the result of fear, not of moral concern. This lack of rational self-management applies to the offender's view of victims as well. The victim's pain, terror, and violation are discounted or minimized by offenders.

WHEN CLERGY ARE THE OFFENDERS

The reality is that clergy are sex offenders. We must move beyond shock if we are to handle cases of clergy sexual malfeasance with justice and caring, and if we expect to root out the causes.

I have listened to the reports of many clergy sex offenders and their victims or partners over the last nineteen years. During this time I have seen some significant trends. First, there is a greater incidence of clergy sexual malfeasance, and the percentage of clergy succumbing is still growing. Only part of this trend is due to more reporting: victims making accusations and observers speaking up.

Second, with the loss of moral certitude, entitlement and consequence-oriented decision making have become dominant. Entitlement means the presumed right to whatever is desired, even sexual gratification. Consequence-oriented decision making can become the manipulation of options to gain such gratification, as opposed to compliance with moral rules to gain satisfaction through integrity. Both of these trends are being discussed by social commentators because they are now common in our culture. But it is disturbing to note how often clergy use these to excuse moral malfeasance.

Third, the victims of clergy sexual malfeasance are not homogeneous. They are coworkers—ordained and nonordained—children, spouses, family members, parishioners, counselees, and even random acquaintances. These are the primary victims. The secondary victims, whose pain and loss can be devastating, include family, spouse, colleagues, parishioners, the community

at large, the church at large, and the clergyperson herself or himself. This list of victims and the impact of reverberations can be
awesome.

It takes a great effort for victims of clergy to speak up. The
victim's shock, fear, shame, and confusion are clearly aggravated
by the offender's respectable position. When victims of clergy
do speak up, justice is tentative. I was fortunate to have worked
with sensitive, competent, honest, and concerned denominational
executives in most of the clergy sexual malfeasance cases I have
seen. Unfortunately, the cast of characters is not always well
chosen. Cases of dissembling, denial, bumbling, collusion, and
even participation are numerous enough to disillusion the
ingenuous and to encourage investigators to be exhaustive in
probing malfeasance. It is even safe to say that in some cases
tribunals of the church are suspect. From the victim's perspective, the undependability of the church hierarchy in doing justice is double victimization.

Victims of clergy sexual abuse suffer consequences most nearly
identified as betrayal, grief and loss, shame, confusion, rage, and
contamination. Betrayal, because the pastor-parishioner relationship has been violated. Grief and loss, because this pastor can
never truly be a pastor to this person again. (Not only has this
victim lost a pastor, a church home, and faith in God; marriage
and other supportive nurturing resources may also be lost.)
Shame, because sexual intimacy with clergy, whether instigated
or suffered, often implies in the victim's mind the grossest of
moral turpitudes. Confusion, because intimacy and spirituality
are so closely related. (One should be able to experience sex and
spiritual passion with joy rather than through abuse by a spiritual leader.) Rage, because of the power imbalance. A pastor as a
star has position, status, and moral authority as well as some
kind of spiritual expertise. When these unique skills and this
role are used to violate someone vulnerable to such powers, the
natural reaction is rage—either absolute fury or the repressed
rage that fosters depression. Finally, contamination, because the

victim's life is now clouded and distorted by titillating rumor, loss of reputation, voyeuristic sympathy, and mistrust, along with loss of the care and support he or she has a right to receive in the church.

Some victims recover rather quickly from such ordeals. Others suffer lifelong consequences. Their families, spouses, and friends may also suffer deeply if the victim experiences mental disorder, economic loss, and ill health. Concern for any victims of sexual malfeasance should include providing confidential and trauma-specific counsel and therapy, for the devastation is usually considerable. Serious depression is not uncommon. Life losses (career, marriage, reputation, and so forth) may accompany or produce low self-esteem. Post-Traumatic Stress Disorder may be a present or future consequence. This disorder is precipitated by an acutely stressful experience, such as sexual abuse, war, and life-threatening events. The event is relived over and over through intrusive memories called flashbacks. Such repetitions may be so powerful that the person feels hopeless about ending these flashbacks, resulting in apathy and depression. Stress symptoms not present before the trauma appear: insomnia, irritability, loss of concentration, avoidance of cues that remind one of the trauma, and heightened sensitivity to stimuli associated with the memory. This victim's life finally becomes absorbed and enmeshed in the trauma's recurring episodes. Needless to say, this person's life is ruined unless there is therapeutic intervention and treatment.

Secondary Victims

It is likely that there will be secondary victims, or co-victims, that is, persons who suffer from the effects of the behavior or attitude. Such persons typically experience a confusing combination of guilt for what they believe is their share of responsibility for the behavior or attitude, along with anger at the one who initiates them. The victimized spouse, for instance, often feels responsibility for the offending spouse, so the freedom to walk away or stop the pain is seen as unavailable or too costly. The relationship then becomes a prison, in which unwanted pain must repeatedly be suffered.

The trauma of secondary victims is usually less severe than that of primary victims, but may be intense and repetitive, eventually producing severe consequences. Of course, these secondary victims may not know of the offending behavior. They may only see distancing behavior, secretiveness, loss of affection, irritability, or other unexplained changes. Their pain is then complicated by the anxiety of not knowing or by worrisome assumptions. It is sometimes the case, however, that an offending partner (usually a man) not only keeps the offending behavior secret but he may even compensate his partner out of guilt or fear by treating her with unusual affection and support. The penalty for her then becomes not knowing what is really going on, being vulnerable to possible scandalous eruptions, and living an imagined intimacy with a performing partner.

The co-victim role is most apparent in partners in an incompatible marriage, or one in which a spouse is a willing participant in sexual offenses or unusual sexual behavior. The co-victims may not even see themselves as victims, except in the rejection of their behavior by the church and society. It is possible that their understanding of themselves as consenting adults eliminates pain and allows them to enjoy their behavior as normal and satisfying.

The Perpetrator as Victim

It becomes apparent to anyone working with sexual offenders that this person is a victim. It seems strange to speak of the perpetrator or actor as a victim unless we know that he or she was victimized as a child. But it is common for us to bring uncomfortable or tragic consequences down upon our own heads through bad or foolish behavior. I have often heard such a clergyperson say, "If only I had known," or "If only I had taken time to count the cost."

The victimization here is multiple. There may be a life lived in fear of discovery, debilitating guilt and shame, sorrow for pain caused, a ruined career, public disfavor, financial ruin, or even jail. Here I am mixing scandalous malfeasance with sexual behavior that appears to have no victim and may even be viewed as desirable by the initiator. Several of the sexual issues discussed in Part 3 can go on for years without discovery. Masturbation, for example, may not be viewed negatively by many. But victimization still occurs whenever any behavior becomes compulsive and addictive.

A pastor practicing irregular sexual behavior—compulsive masturbation, for example—that he regards as desirable or normal must expend some energy coping with fear, anger, or confusion. Deep inside he may have doubts about his sexuality and moral ethics. He may even expend more energy handling his resentment at those he feels would condemn him if they knew.

PART TWO

CASES IN
CLERGY SEXUAL MALFEASANCE

4

SEXUAL ADDICTION

Addiction to sex can be manifested as clergy malfeasance in many ways: affairs, incest, pedophilia, rape, sexual harassment. I see addiction as closely correlating to the star factor. Nature and nurture, of course, play a part. Genetic factors seem to influence a person's predisposition to addiction; overstimulation, high-intensity living, and "entitlement thinking" also contribute to the formation of addictive behavior. But I have found that the environmental factors so encourage clergy malfeasance that all clergy are vulnerable to addictive behavior, especially sexually based ones. The star factor is the precursor. Thus the case featured in this chapter illustrates the dynamics behind other chapters in this part.

A PASTOR WITH MULTIPLE PARTNERS

A pastor in his thirties began to phone our office regularly and expect to talk to me at length about the problems he said he was having with his wife, who would not respond to his sexual demands the way he wanted. He kept asking me to tell him ways to get his wife to conform to his desires. His narcissistic tendencies were obvious. I encouraged him to make an office appointment, and he did.

He was so intent on telling his story, with vivid details, and with urgency in asking for ways to control his wife, that we had trouble even accomplishing our simple registration process. Quickly he adapted to a pattern of regular appointments and usually tried to get the next appointment set sooner than the previous one. My gentle but firm insistence on a regularized process usually reassured him, and he quickly transferred an obvious dependence to me. A pattern developed in our appointments. He would tell me over and over the latest episodes of his wife resisting his inordinate sexual demands. He had little insight into this pattern or its consequences for his wife. My statements of reality did not seem to touch him.

As I encouraged him to discuss his daily life and his work, he invariably did so with sexual references. Then he began to tell of two affairs he was having. He told of the women he worked with—the church secretary, a woman leader in the congregation, and other women in the town, all of whom he found fascinating, and who, according to his report, responded to his advances.

After several appointments in which this pattern was repeated, he became somewhat bored with it, and frustrated that I was not giving advice on how to change his wife's responses. This was the time to suggest including his wife in our counseling process. He agreed, obviously intent on hooking her into his purposes. She joined us with a wary and guarded demeanor. It was obvious that she was listening and watching me carefully to see if she could trust me, and whether or not I would simply agree to the pressure he put on her. Soon she began sobbing and saying a phrase I was to hear from her often, "He never stops. I try, but it's never enough. Why can't he be normal!" Her anguish was obvious and real.

The wife then presented a painful description of her daily ordeal. Whenever he came home, he started some kind of sex play. He constantly wanted her to undress for him, and he often tried to take pictures of parts of her body. Even when the children were around his behavior was highly suggestive. At night the ritual was always the same. No matter how tired she was or how much she protested, he demanded full sexual freedom with her. Even when she yielded, in hopes of satisfying him and getting the pressure off for a day or two, he barely let up in his demands.

The husband did not contest his wife's viewpoint. He simply started to make his case, explaining that his life was stressful, and sexual activity was very relieving for him. What could be more natural than to have sex with his wife! He completed his case by saying that he never abused her, and that she ought to be flattered by his desire for her body. He even reported how often he brought her flowers and candy, and how much he helped with parenting and household chores. He apparently expected the logic of his arguments to win the case for him.

I suggested that they become part of our marriage therapy group; they agreed. A group we had recently established, composed of seven other couples, accepted them readily. All were professionals, but this was the only clergy couple. As it happened, the group included two recovering alcoholics, a dynamic, self-confessed workaholic, two couples troubled by compulsive money-management habits, two women who were depressive personality types, and one man who was aggressively fundamentalist in religion. Not surprisingly, the group had begun to focus on the problem of addiction. They almost unanimously zeroed in on this clergyman and quickly decided that he was addicted to sex.

It was a stunning revelation to the clergyman. His wife, however, quickly agreed with the verdict. After a heated discussion of what he considered unfair and untrue charges against him, the pastor's defenses began to crumble. He agreed to continue in the group and to pursue individual appointments with me, dealing with his sexual behavior as an addiction.

In individual counseling the pastor came to understand some contributing factors to his addiction, including obsessive anxiety and silence regarding sexuality in the family he grew up in. His rebellion against this prudish view of human sexuality, his developed habit of using sex as a stress reducer, and the sex drive of an energetic man combined to promote this addiction. From this new understanding, he moved on to change.

He ended his affairs, developed a strong interest in golf, and found that masturbation helped him lessen sexual pressure on his wife. He also developed significant spiritual disciplines in his life, which undergirded his change and obviously deepened his pastoral ministry. He became part of a regular clergy peer group. I encouraged him to express intimacy toward his wife that did not include sex or involve manipulation to gain sexual access. He came to see that nearly all of his behaviors toward her had previously been guided by a sexual agenda, which severely limited the potential richness of a relationship with her.

COMMENTARY

Recent insights in psychotherapy conclude that sexual practices can be compulsive or addictive. This perspective takes the experience of chemical abuse, primarily alcoholism, as a model to be applied to sexual practices that appear to be out of control and enslaving for the person who practices them. Treatment, support groups, and recovery regimens closely resemble what is now established practice in aiding alcoholics to recover normal life without the use of alcohol.

There is value in this perspective. First, it raises our awareness of a formerly undefined malady. It really is true that a significant number of persons finds a particular sexual practice to be so pleasurable, comforting, and capable of temporarily reducing stress that it is indulged obsessively, becoming the focus of a person's behavior beyond what is assumed to be normal human sexual behavior. The contemporary sexual revolution has contributed to this problem. In society as a whole, consciousness of human sexuality, openly practiced sexual behavior, and the constant use of sexual stimulation in the marketplace have become generally acceptable. When something as stimulating and pleasurable as sex becomes readily available, with little control or penalty, it is certain to hook vulnerable persons into addictive consumption.

A second insight from this perspective is the awareness that nearly anything can become addictive. Until now popular opinion and even clinical theory generally assumed that only certain substances could become addictive. Some materials have an innate biochemical capability of enslaving the body to their use. This fostered the commonsense notion that if a person avoided such substances, addiction would not occur, and it perpetuated the myth that only morally weak persons allowed themselves to become addicted to these substances. It is now understood, however, that all of us have the potential for becoming addicted to various substances, practices, and even ideas.

A third insight from this perspective is that certain personality types are more vulnerable to certain addictions than others. The rebel, for example, is likely to choose to consume substances or engage in practices considered outrageous to authority figures and fascinating by peers. A trendsetter, jet-setter, or member of an in-group has similar characteristics. Continuing use establishes a habit, and habits are seldom discarded when there are strong rewards (reinforcement) for the habit. All persons, however, have unique vulnerabilities to becoming addicted.

A fourth insight is the importance of having stress-reduction mechanisms and substances available for handling high anxiety. Our society promotes and in some settings demands high-intensity functioning. If we are to believe the lore about the good old days, previous generations rested, watched sunsets, talked, and in general led less anxious lives. They had less stress and therefore required fewer stress-reducing agents. Contemporary society has more stress; it therefore requires more stress reducers. Many of us even induce anxiety regularly, becoming addicted to our own adrenalin. In this state we do not perceive ourselves as addicted, for we have come to identify this state as normal. Relaxation and lack of stimulation then produce their own reactive anxiety, for these are perceived as abnormal. The use of stress reducers therefore also becomes part of what is perceived as normal, while the person takes a certain pride in surviving the extraordinary stress. It is an acknowledged fact that addicted persons can no longer imagine themselves and their world without their addictive agent. This is one of the tasks for recovery—to reconceptualize the self and the world without the addictive agent and without the need for it. (For a full discussion of this phenomenon, see chapters 4 and 8 of my book, *Lord, Don't Let Me Be Bored* [Philadelphia: Westminster Press, 1986].)

A final insight is in regard to treatment and recovery. It is now assumed in some psychotherapeutic circles that treatment requires a carefully controlled "drying out" period—a time span in which the addict is not allowed to use the addicting agent, is taught the etiology of addiction, and begins to learn to live without it. Treatment must continue long enough for the physical and emotional system of the victim to become disabused and return to what is considered by the treatment facilitators to be a normal condition. This intense treatment period includes introduction to an Alcoholics Anonymous type of support group. Such a group process is continued after the intense treatment period, as a bridge from addictive to nonaddictive behavior. For many recovering addicts, the support group becomes a regular part of their lives. They are told that one never fully recovers from an addiction, is never "cured"; the habit is only arrested. The addict continues to be vulnerable and is encouraged to think of himself or herself thereafter as continually recovering.

5

AFFAIRS

My experience with clergy indicates their extramarital sexual activities or affairs have increased, as have the general public's. Fifteen years ago clergy affairs were rare and scandalous. In 1988 approximately 18 percent of my clergy counselees had had or were involved in affairs. They included among the contributing factors parents who had affairs, peers having affairs, easy opportunities, loss of moral certitude, and unhappiness with their marriages. A ripple effect seems to have occurred from the beginning of the contemporary surge in clergy divorces. Once clergy with unhappy marriages noticed that the sky did not fall when their peers got divorced, they decided not to put up with their unhappy marriages any longer. Few clergy having affairs stop them voluntarily. They typically end with scandal, career moves, or the partner withdrawing.

A PASTOR AND AN EXECUTIVE

A young, single, and childless clergywoman made an appointment with me when she was in her first full-time pastoral position. It was a small parish in a small town. She was bright, competent, and idealistic. As with most young pastors, she imagined her task was to change this church into what it ought to be.

She came to our first appointment with reports of parishioners' uncooperativeness and her own failures. After several such stories and tears, she agreed to a series of appointments to explore these issues.

In subsequent appointments we quickly discovered that she had intense romantic feelings for a denominational executive and was seeing him regularly. The relationship included sex. She was not embarrassed by discussing their sexual relationship, although I knew the man would have been. In fact, she complained that there was not enough intimacy and sex. His busy schedule made it difficult for him to set aside time for them to be alone together.

Our appointments centered on her bittersweet relationship with this church executive. I asked her if she saw the significance of this shift in agenda, because it was not the presenting problem of our first appointment. She indicated that this pattern showed her how much she wanted a primary intimate relationship and marriage. She had not wanted to admit this to herself. Then she noted that being single and relatively isolated in a small town left her without some important support resources; so she had come to depend on her relationship to this man for emotional support.

The young woman decided to make more contact with close friends—by phone, by letters, and, when possible, by meeting them regularly for social activities. After doing this for a few weeks, she felt more relaxed and better able to come to terms with the realities of her congregation and community. But she was also realizing that without a primary intimate relationship, marriage and family, her professional ministry would be less and less satisfying.

We agreed that she would invite the executive to join her for the counseling appointments. At first he resisted; then he made an appointment but did not show up. One day, they walked in together. Our first joint appointment was spent with her trying to tell him that she could not go on without him, while he squirmed in embarrassment and tried to defend his behavior.

I suggested an individual appointment for him and a tentative follow-up joint appointment. They agreed.

In his appointment the executive discussed his embarrassment and his guilt. Then he began to tell me his own history of two earlier marriages that ended in divorce. It was obvious that he had unresolved issues, so we set another individual appointment. The woman agreed to this arrangement. The man had ten appointments in which we dealt with his grief and loss, his anger at the church and God, his embarrassment and guilt, his theological and spiritual pilgrimage, and his feelings for this woman. Then it was time for the woman to join us again.

After discussing how both were experiencing this counseling process and each other during this period, they settled into a serious discussion of the possibility of marriage. After several months of discussion, they agreed that marriage would not work for them. He was unwilling to give up his career pattern and commitments to invest in a marriage and family as she wanted; she was unwilling to give up her career plans and her vision of marriage and family to become the supportive wife to his executive role. With much sorrow, they agreed to end the relationship. I had several individual appointments with each as they began their grief and loss resolution and thought about future intimate relationships.

A PASTOR AND HIS SECRETARY

Another of our clergy cases presented a more traditional version of an affair, involving the typical form of adultery.

A midlife clergy couple walked in for their first appointment. After exchanging pleasantries, they sat down. Some gentle banter followed in which they tried to decide which one would tell me why they had come. Finally he said, "It's my daughter," and began to cry. It took a long time, with her weeping, too, before he could say that their daughter, who had just graduated from high school, had moved into the off-campus apartment of a seminary student. The student and their daughter were not married. "What is the ministry coming to?" he sobbed. "My daughter living in sin with a future pastor, while he is studying how to be a pastor!"

Then he told how the shock of his daughter's nonchalant announcement had made him realize what he was doing in his own life and ministry. For years, during a successful, long pastorate at a good church, he had been committing adultery with the church secretary, who also was married. They would go to religious meetings together, have afternoon trysts in his office, and be openly affectionate with each other. Everyone seemed to know what was going on, including his wife and daughter. But no one said anything about it publicly. After all, the church was doing well, and no one was complaining. It was as if everyone were mesmerized into inaction, waiting for a disaster to make the decision no one wanted to make.

When his daughter made her announcement, he said he "came to his senses." He realized now what he had been doing to himself, the secretary, his wife, the congregation, the ministry, and now his daughter. The clergy couple had resolved to stay together and work on their marriage. They had gone to the secretary and her husband. All four decided to end the adulterous relationship and work on their marriages. The pastor and his wife now wanted assistance in reshaping their marriage, and they wanted to know what to do about their daughter.

In subsequent appointments, we went through a process of confession and forgiveness, and we developed a pattern for their marriage that pleased them. The congregation seemed to breathe a sigh of relief, and made no scandal. The daughter, however, did not respond to their pleadings.

COMMENTARY

Several factors likely affect the rising incidence of extramarital sex or affairs. Clergy are human beings. They are affected by the seductiveness of increased sexual promiscuity. Denominational discipline has been relaxed; theology is in disarray. The clergy divorce rate has climbed. An increasing number of women and men feel free to express their sexual feelings; and there has been a substantial increase of women and single persons in clergy ranks. More clergy spouses—once confined to the parsonage— are involved in satisfying jobs and careers; home is no longer the only center for satisfaction. None of these factors is an excuse, but all are additional reasons for the increase we are seeing in clergy sexual affairs.

The settings for affairs are changing also. There is more time, money, and opportunity for clergy to attend conferences and continuing education events. Some of the increased sexual activities occur in such settings. The absence of the clergy spouse from the parsonage, the increase of single and divorced clergy living there, and the lessening attention laity pay to what goes on in the manse make this setting more likely for affairs.

The rationalizing that takes place in clergy affairs is noteworthy. Both conservative and liberal clergy more frequently separate the sexual part of their lives from the rest. Clergy frequently admit their affairs to me with little apparent guilt. Some have even adjusted the moral tenets of their theology to justify their behavior. Some feel justified in having an affair because it is limited to one person and because they feel deep love for that person. Still others justify their behavior with a sense of entitlement. They feel they have a right to sexual satisfaction. If they do not find it with their marriage partner, they assume that they have a right to seek it elsewhere.

My experience in counseling with clergy indicates that relatively few of them plan to have an affair. It usually sneaks up on them and catches them off guard—at a conscious level. Over a period of time in counseling, however, it is usually not difficult to see the pattern of vulnerability that developed and that sets them up for the affair. The vulnerability usually begins with lack of intimacy with the marriage partner, or the loss of an intimate and supportive circle of relatives and friends. As this breakdown continues or grows, the clergyperson begins to starve emotionally. Pastoral relationships with loving parishioners do not always help, because such relationships are usually half-intimacies. Parishioners can have their intimacy needs met by the pastor, but he is seldom free to open up completely with them or have this sharing reciprocated.

As the intimacy breakdown continues, the pastor begins to feel resentment—"She doesn't support my ministry"; anger— "He's not there when I need him"; frustration—"She's never willing to do it my way"; hurt—"He acts bored with me"; rejec- tion—"She spends more time with the kids than with me"; and disenchantment—"He's not the person I married." If these feel- ings cannot be discussed and satisfactory changes negotiated, it is only a matter of time until one or both partners slide into resignation, seek a divorce, or find intimacy elsewhere.

Another common pattern of vulnerability is the sustained work or counseling relationship. Pastors often say that it dawned on them one day how much they enjoyed the company of a co- worker. Soon they begin planning to be together and talking about their feelings for each other. The outcome is predictable.

Pastors can set themselves up for affairs in many ways. Most frequent are these: not investing in their primary intimate rela- tionship; arranging house calls, meetings, and activities that set up or ignore sexual possibilities; allowing themselves to become exhausted or bored; paying inordinate attention to pornography; allowing themselves to develop and expand sexual fantasies; beginning to rationalize inappropriate sexual activities; forget- ting or ignoring spiritual and professional accountability and integrity; believing that if they fall in love with a person other than a spouse, they have no power to control this passion; believing that discovery, pain, and punishment for affairs hap- pen only to other clergy; and believing that they are entitled to sexual gratification no matter how they have to get it.

It is tempting to believe that if pastors keep fired up spiritu- ally, affairs will cease to occur. I heartily endorse spiritual disci- pline and enthusiasm, but I do not find that this alone keeps pastors from having affairs. (I could fill a book with stories of pastors who are "on fire for the Lord" while having affairs.) It is also tempting to fall into the sexist trap of believing that if wives of clergymen followed the "total woman" approach and devoted themselves to their husbands, affairs would cease. The value of devotion and commitment between the spouses is unquestionable, but this is not the solution. This, consequently, is the basis for my earlier plea for more self-awareness, self-care, and personalized theological anchors.

6

INCEST

Incest is common. It occurs in privileged as well as underprivileged families, usually in the home. The perpetrator can be a parent, brother, sister, or any other relative; most often it is a male. Immaturity and irresponsibility, along with an early history of fascination with sex, rationalization of the incestuous behavior, and secrecy in personal life frequently characterize the perpetrator. A significant number of those who act incestuously toward others were themselves so treated as children.

Incest signals self-distortions and boundary distortions. The perpetrator's need for affection plays on a child's trust and fear of authority figures and the child's need to be loved. Such play is not innocent because it causes trauma and often destroys trust and respect, produces a distorted sexual self-image, and makes it terribly difficult for the child to become an adult who can have normal intimate relationships.

A DAD AND HIS DAUGHTERS

"He kept excusing his sexual advances toward our daughters by calling them 'sex education.' He would say things like: 'You should be happy that I'm willing to teach my daughters about sex'; or, 'Don't be so prudish. I have to help them be sexually liberated for the kind of world they're growing up in.' I knew something was wrong, but I felt too hurt, too afraid, too angry to do anything about it."

These were the words of a midlife pastor's wife. For several visits she recited, in a numb monotone, the random details and chronology of this pastor's sexual abuse of their daughters. It was not until the fourth appointment that she was able to break down and sob out some of the excruciating emotions she had been feeling for a couple of years. Then we had a chance to open up the whole pattern of his sexual manipulations and his abuse of these daughters.

She first became aware of the problem in her family when she noticed the long, silent periods while her husband was in the bathroom giving each girl her nightly bath before he put her to bed (they had agreed, as the girls got beyond the toddler stage, that they should both participate actively in all the duties of parenting). She was only vaguely aware of uneasy feelings for a long time. Her uneasiness, however, turned to anxious concern as she asked her husband if he ever had erotic feelings about his daughters, and why he made such passionate love to her on Thursday and Sunday nights, the nights that he bathed their daughters. His irritable response did not seem appropriate.

One evening she stopped outside the closed bathroom door and heard the daughter inside with her husband say something like, "Ouch, Daddy, that hurts!" She pushed the door open and saw her husband sexually fondling the girl. Though she was stunned, she made a calm remark about bedtime and left the bathroom. Later that night, when she and her husband were in bed, she asked about the bathroom episode. That was when he began his remarks about his sexual behavior with the girls being good sex education. She felt intense surges of anger, hurt, fear, and confusion.

Then came revulsion. One day she watched a television talk show about sexual abuse. As she heard the stories of several women who had been abused by their fathers while growing up, and as she learned about the emotional distortions this caused in their lives, a feeling of revulsion came over her so strongly that she lost her breakfast. After the revulsion came anger— anger mixed with guilt. She heard these women say that when they told their mothers about the sexual abuse, their mothers only tried to calm them or told them they were inviting it. The abuse continued.

This was the turning point. That night the woman confronted her husband with the fury of an enraged parent. When he tried his usual excuses, she escalated to accusations and ultimatums. When he did not respond, she threatened to go to his bishop with the story. Then she stormed out of their bedroom and spent a sleepless night in the spare bedroom.

The next morning her husband warned her not to tell the bishop or anyone else, because this would only lead to disaster for all of them. Her day was spent in emotional turmoil. When her husband returned from his church meeting that night, she told him that either he must go with her to my office or she would take the risk of telling the bishop. He shocked her by saying, "Go ahead and tell him, and see what it gets us!" That was when she knew she was in a double bind. She could not tell the bishop, and she could not let the abuse continue. The next morning she phoned my office and scheduled an appointment.

The most difficult part of the process was strategizing. The woman felt trapped, and her emotions of rage, hurt, and confusion were turning inward. This created a block to planning effective action. Over and over she repeated, "I'm not sure what to do."

In her appointments she now began to consider a word I used several times in reflecting her thinking back to her. The word was "permission." I said, "It sounds as if you need permission to act on one of your strategies." She did not accept this idea at first. But then she reflected that she was already taking action— she was holding the feelings and energy inside. This, she began to understand, is what she had learned to do over many years. She reflected on her mother's silent suffering in the face of her father's dominance, and she noted the gender programming she had accepted, which led her to believe women should not be assertive. She remembered a favorite aunt whom everyone seemed to admire, an elegant and sophisticated woman admired for her ladylike demeanor and behavior. In her mind, there was a strong connection among elegance and silent suffering and the admiration of others. It took several appointments to sort out these feelings and memories and to contemplate the possible strategies.

There was a look of determination on her face as she arrived for our appointment one day. She announced immediately that she had decided to go to the bishop with her story. Then she immediately stared at my face and became silent. I said nothing. After a long silence, she said, "Well?" I replied, "Well?" She said, "Well, what do you think?" After another long silence, she sobbed. After regaining her composure, she said, "It's very hard, you know." I nodded and remained silent. "I am outraged by his behavior. I'm suffering with my daughters. And I'm afraid of what will happen to them as they grow up. And now I'm considering taking action that will probably result in our disgrace and my husband's leaving the ministry."

She didn't cry now; she just stared at me. I said, "Wouldn't it be nice if someone would do this for you and guarantee that everything would turn out beautifully?" She smiled feebly and remained silent for a while. Then she said, "I'm going to do it— alone if I have to. I know that I'm not alone, but I sure feel alone." At the close of this appointment I asked her to bring a written statement next time that would indicate clearly her chosen plan of action. She left with a very troubled look on her face.

At the beginning of the next appointment, she immediately took a typed statement out of her purse, read it to me, and then stared at it silently. She tried to hand it to me, but I asked her to date it and sign it. She did so very slowly. Then I said, "Who are the witnesses to this signature?" She stared off into space, and then slowly said, "You, my daughters, God, my mother, my father, my friends Sylvia and Marcie. I guess everyone in the whole world will soon be my witnesses!" I said, "Is your husband a witness to your signature on this statement?" "Yes," she said emphatically. I asked, "Do you think he would join you here or with some other counselor if you showed him this paper?" "I don't know," she said. "It's worth a try, isn't it?" "Let's set another appointment for you, and in the meantime you decide whether or not you will show him this paper, and whether or not you can accept him as a partner in handling this matter."

She came to the next appointment with a tired face. She said she had shown the paper to her husband and he had been furious. After he calmed down, he agreed to come for an appointment. They are still in counseling at this writing.

COMMENTARY

Incest disturbs the whole family system. Child victims often feel guilt and a confused need for love; the spouse is put in a double bind. When the incest becomes known, the perpetrator requires restraint, discipline, counseling, and reconciliation; the victims need protection, loving acceptance, and counseling.

The pastor who engages in incest does not typically show in his sexual behavior the same compulsive-addictive patterns as the pedophile. His abuse is a function of opportunity, normal parental love, and often undisciplined sexual appetite. My experience indicates that the incestuous pastor, when he has confronted, corrected, and demonstrated accountability for his sexual behavior, can be trusted again with his own children and the children of others. This generally involves accepting complete responsibility for his sexual behavior with his child (or children), accounting for the variables that promote his offending behavior and correcting these, and reducing whatever sexual arousal he may experience with underage children. Nevertheless, neither the perpetrator nor the victims will ever be the same again. They may heal and grow as persons, but the scars and residue of incest will remain and will never lose the power to disrupt lives and distort intimacy.

Incest is a secret problem. In the case that we have considered, the pastor was secretive; so were his daughters and, for a time, their mother. Secretiveness supports and suggests shame, guilt, and fear. Breaking the secrecy pattern can be an important element in correcting the behavior because perpetrators not infrequently engage in other inappropriate sexual behaviors. It is even more important, however, to deal with the powerful emotional dynamics—the shame, guilt, and fear. These feelings not only are occasioned by incest, they also contribute to its continuation.

The shocking realization that incest occurs in a large number of families has numbed our society. Denial that it could ever happen in our own family is a common and understandable reaction. But it could and it does. It happens in church families, and some of the perpetrators are clergy.

One might think that the church would respond quickly to the slightest suspicion of incest, and that it would deal decisively and caringly with any substantiated instance of it. Instead, the church tends to turn its head. When the perpetrator is a clergyperson, the church often engages in exquisite self-torture. Intent on saving face, hierarchy and laity frequently collude in an elaborate charade aimed at warding off shame and scandal. To protect the charade, perpetrators and victims are subjected to numerous and inventive techniques of avoidance.

Surely we can do better than this. When it has been discovered that a clergyperson is perpetrating incest, there are caring ways to respond. The incest must be terminated immediately. The victims (in our case, not only the daughters but also the wife/mother) need validation, protection, competent therapy, and loving support. The perpetrator needs to be disciplined and counseled. The community of faith must be led through its normal reactions into sensitivity and spiritual growth, if they learn about it.

7

PEDOPHILIA

Pedophilia is the erotic attraction of an adult to prepubescent children and the use of children for sexual gratification. Such sexual abuse of children is much more common than we had thought. The incidence is high not only among Roman Catholic priests but also among Protestant clergy (about 2 or 3 percent are offenders). Current data indicate that offenders are almost exclusively adult males. Boys are victimized five times as often as girls.

About 25 percent of abusers were abused as children. The typical offender reports feeling "different" as a child, and may have adopted mannerisms that either express or hide that feeling. Offenders often have a history of precocious sexual fantasizing and frequently augment current fantasies with substance abuse. They tend to rationalize and minimize their behavior and its consequences.

A FRIEND OF BOYS

A suave, handsome male pastor in his mid-fifties came into my office, introduced himself in an affable and articulate manner, and fell silent. When he began to speak again, it took him a while to get to the point. I heard about a "deep, dark secret" and about how frightened he was that its revelation would ruin his job, his marriage, his reputation. Then it came out. This pastor had recently been followed by the parent of a young boy whom he was driving to a Cub Scout meeting. If he had not noticed the father in his rearview mirror, the pastor would have taken the boy from the meeting to the local Dairy Queen for a treat, and from there to the park for oral sex. Finishing his story, the pastor looked like a man who had been rescued from certain death. "Thank God," he whispered. "Thank God I saw the car."

He seemed somewhat relieved to have said it out loud and to have assured himself that he had not been caught. He spent the rest of the hour telling me about several young boys with whom he had had sex in the several parishes he had served. There seemed to be some remorse, and there were brief expressions of shame and guilt; but mostly he expressed relief to be talking about it. At the end of the appointment he quickly pulled himself together and walked out of the office with aplomb.

The next appointment was spent on life and generational history. He believed his father was gay and oriented to little boys, but had never seen any evidence. He had had a couple of sexual experiences with an uncle when he visited his farm one summer. He recalled these experiences with little demonstration of feeling. Toward the end of the hour he began telling me about a favorite pastor when he was in upper grades and junior high school. The next appointment he told me more. He obviously enjoyed the memories of his relationship with this man, which included oral and anal sex.

He had done well in school and gone right through college and seminary with singleness of purpose, as if he could hardly wait to be a pastor. He had married a college girlfriend who was intent on a career in nursing. They had two children but little sexual intimacy. He had never molested his son and was not even tempted. But young boys in church were a constant attraction, and several became his victims. His wife seemed to suspect and warned him once that if he ever got into sexual trouble, she would leave with the children immediately. She seemed content to concentrate on her successful career and the children, but she most often joined him to appear at church events where both were expected.

There was a significant pattern in this pastor's relationship with boys. He spent lots of time building a friendly, trusting relationship with each boy before having sex. He even reported that each of the boys loved him dearly and engaged in sex willingly. None had ever reported him to parents or authorities; he did not seem worried that they would! It was not until he was followed by a boy's father that fear seized him and caused him to seek help.

Counseling this pastor posed significant problems, both for him and for me. The now-standard law requiring the reporting of abuse of children had not been passed. But after we found ways for him to realize the enormity of his abuse of these boys, and had established a measure of self-control, we discussed the strategy for helping these boys recover.

We found that the boys in previous parishes were grown, and all but one were seemingly functioning normally. That one had been in and out of jail and therapy for several years. It took several months for the pastor to make discreet inquiries to gather this information. There had been two victims in this present parish. With one boy there had been no sex, only a growing relationship. He agreed to work toward getting this boy to transfer his church relationship to another responsible youth adviser. This left us with one boy to get into therapy, and it was the boy whose father had tailed the pastor. The pastor discovered that this boy's father had some psychological problems, with a characteristic paranoia. The boy had been physically abused at home and had a poor record in school. There was a good mental health center in the town, and the boy and his whole family were established in counseling there by the time this pastor resigned to take another church.

Before he moved, I insisted that the pastor establish some controls on his behavior. His wife finally joined us and readily agreed to assist him in watching for signs of weakness and a recurrence of the abuse. I asked him if he wanted anything further from me. He said he wanted me to be ready to tell his whole story to his denominational executive if his wife contacted me and told of any recurrence. I told him that I would be glad to talk over possibilities if such an occasion occurred. We reviewed again the seriousness of the sexual abuse he had committed. I discussed his options again, from going to each boy and family and confessing and doing what he could to repair the damage, to assisting through anonymous prayers, to letting the situations alone and doing all he could to help the church deal with such abuses.

COMMENTARY

Pedophilia is distinguished by some authorities from ephebophilia, sexual attraction to and use of pubescent youths. Research has not yet clarified all the distinguishing characteristics of these disorders. Pedophilia, however, appears to focus on young boys who because of their innocence can be treated as objects—as if they were young dolls to be toyed with, manipulated, and examined—for the abuser's pleasure. Undeveloped physical characteristics apparently allow abusers to fantasize their own innocence and satyrize compliant bodies. The abusers seem as intent upon active and adoring relationships with boys as upon the sexual behavior. The abuser pretends that his victim participates for mutual gratification, and he wants to act as if this were a healthy relationship. The abuser will often take a boy under his wing and act as a mentor. Such boys perceive a lack of affection and support from their parents and find a replacement in an affectionate adult male, who often seduces them but who gives them enduring attention and support. Not all boys yield willingly to either the pedophiliac or the ephebophiliac. But such abusive men seem to have a talent for finding boys who will be responsive. When these characteristics are understood, it is not hard to see the reason that therapy with such men and their victims is so difficult. It should also help us recognize that such men, even after long therapy, should never be allowed to have private and authority-figure relationships with young boys again.

Pedophilia (the term usually used in popular discussion of both forms of abuse) is a topic much in the news these days. It can have terrible consequences for the victim—distorted self-image, confused sexual identity, inability to form healthy relationships, often resulting in another sexually abusive adult. The suicide rate among victims of abuse is unusually high. The wonder, perhaps, is that many victims somehow manage to develop rather normally and live relatively happy lives. For all, however, there is a deep, dark secret inside them, potentially able to distort significantly their lives and relationships.

The causes of pedophilia and ephebophilia are not clear, although genetic factors and early childhood experiences—including abuse—seem to be involved. Abusers are almost always male, more frequently heterosexual in adult sexual orientation in cases of ephebophilia but predominantly homosexual in adult sexual orientation in cases of pedophilia. (There seems to be some connection between this fact and the percentage of pedophilia involving Roman Catholic clergy, but even here the causal factors are not clearly known.)

What is clear is that many children are sexually abused, and clergy are involved far more often than we had suspected. We should be alert to danger signals and take responsible action when we see them. The signals include obviously strange patterns of behavior by an adult playing with children and reports or body language in which children hint at their discomfort in the presence of that adult. Other signals include singling out one (or more) boys for loving attention, inappropriate touching, gift giving, shared "secrets," too much time together alone, and denial of any special relationship. None of these behaviors is necessarily an indication in itself, but in clusters they often indicate an inappropriate relationship or abuse. The observation of such signals should be verified, ideally by discussing them first with the child and then, if indicated, with the clergyperson. If this is impossible for any reason, including the observer's hesitance to approach the matter, someone in a position to help must be notified.

There is a risk in all this—the risk of allegations against the innocent, of witch hunts, even of a breakdown in the traditional trust of clergy. On their part, innocent clergy might find it difficult to relax and act naturally with children. It is essential, therefore, that people be sensitive and objective as they move from one stage to another in the process. But the risk must be taken, and clergy must learn to accept uncomfortable inquiries as signs of human concern.

Verification of pedophilia or ephebophilia demands immediate separation of the offender from all victims—actual or potential. There can be no question of moving a pastor to another church where the same kind of situation will arise. Treatment of the disorder includes intensive therapy and carefully restricted vocational and leisure activities. Recidivism is high; continued monitoring of the offender is necessary. Clergy who suffer from this terrible distortion of sexuality can live productive lives, but there can be no thought of things getting back to normal.

The victims of abuse by clergy must be given special attention. Children have come to church, only then to be mistreated. The church in which this has happened cannot waste energy attempting to save face or telling itself that it cannot have happened here. It did. Now the challenge is to be available to the victims, with all the compassion and competent help that they need. Occasionally now some streetwise youths are able to use clergy vulnerability and public outrage with child abuse for their own sinister purposes. But accusations and danger signals must always be taken seriously, because they typically indicate abuse.

8

RAPE

The stereotypical rapist is an angry man who enacts his violence on women in a parking lot or alley at knife- or gunpoint. Clergy rapists—because of the star factor's power differential—are able to force themselves on their victims in a rather calm manner with no weapons and little resistance. In fact, the victims are not even sure that what occurred was rape until feelings of rage or violation surface later. Here, as in other cases, the perspective of the victim is key. Not only have I been involved at the request of the victim but I have also learned that the victim's perspective—being used for sexual pleasure at the demand of the other while not receiving any pleasure or satisfaction in return—establishes this as a clergy sexual malfeasance. The following case, while seemingly unusual, is typical of the cases I have treated.

A PASTOR, HIS WIFE, AND HER FEMALE FRIEND

The wife of a clergyman made the initial contact with our office. In the first appointment, she indicated that something was bothering her. "I feel angry, confused, and guilty all at the same time," she said. Then she told of how her husband had become domineering in their sexual relationship. "When we were first married," she said, "he was warm and tender and sensitive to my needs. But when the babies began to come, and I began to worry about becoming pregnant again and often was too exhausted at night to feel ready for sexual intimacy, I found ways to resist his initiatives quite often. I didn't intend to deprive him or control our sexual relationship. It just sort of happened, and didn't seem all that unusual to me.

"But I'll never forget that night," she said, "the night he came home from a church-sponsored workshop on sexuality. He said he was sick and tired of me controlling our sex life, and he was going to have normal sex whether I liked it or not. He's not a violent or abusive man," she said. "So I wasn't frightened, just sort of shocked. And I realized that I had become somewhat selfish in terms of sexual expression—maybe even dominating, from his perspective. I remember feeling guilty and thinking I really ought to let him have sex whether I felt like it or not. So we began to have sex just about any time he wanted it. Sometimes I enjoyed it, but more and more I just felt like a dutiful wife.

"Then something happened. I still can't believe it. My closest woman friend, who is married, was visiting me for a couple of days. One hot day about a month ago, my husband came home early and found me and my friend sitting around in our swimsuits. We had taken our two children to the community pool, and now they were upstairs having their naps." Her husband had suggested that they have a cocktail. While they sat around drinking, he began to make sexually suggestive remarks; the woman did the same. Soon the pastor announced that he was going to get into a swimsuit, too. When he returned to the recreation room, he was naked.

"My friend and I were surprised, but since we had all been good friends for a long time, and considered ourselves open and free, we weren't shocked or afraid," she said. "My husband made some playful sexual remarks, then he went over to the couch beside my friend. He reached out and took off her swimsuit, pushed her down on her back, climbed on top, and had intercourse with her. She didn't object, although she surely didn't initiate sex," the woman concluded.

When he was done, he went over to his wife and led her to the couch. Her friend got up; her husband then stretched his wife out on the davenport and had intercourse with her. "I didn't particularly like what was going on," she said. "But I was fascinated by seeing an aggressive, lustful man in action. After he was satisfied, we put our swimsuits back on and sat around talking. It was a couple of days later, after my friend had left, that I began to feel angry and hurt," she said. "The more I thought about it, the more I realized that what had happened that day with my friend, and what my husband had been doing to me, made me feel used and abused. I no longer had any say in our sexual activity. And he seemed to feel that he had a right to have sex any time and with anyone he wanted."

She then told me that her friend had phoned sometime after the swimsuit incident. She said her friend expressed great confusion and asked her what in the world happened that day. They discussed the new morality, sexual sophistication, and the intimacies appropriate to close friendships. They had both agreed that this was unwanted sexual dominance by a male. They even discussed how to confront him, but could not come up with a satisfying strategy.

Finally, she told me that she had seen a TV program about date rape—a male's insistence on having sex with a date or good friend whether or not she wanted it. The women on the program reported feeling trapped into sex because they liked the man and because their friends would think they were weird if they complained. This, she was convinced, had become the story of her life and the explanation of what had happened to her friend.

I told her that these are the very reasons many of us are calling this type of sexual intercourse by the name of rape. For it is rape when one partner demands and has pleasure while the other partner does not. It is rape when the most private and personal parts of one person's body are used by another without appreciation, sensitivity, or giving anything in return. It is rape when physical intimacy is not shared lovingly.

After a couple of appointments at our office, the woman convinced her husband to join her in counseling. He was somewhat embarrassed, but immediately began to explain why what he was doing was not wrong. After all, he had been patient and accepting of his wife's dominance for years. Now it was his turn. Anyway, times had changed. He was so intent upon explaining his behavior that I had difficulty getting him to go through our registration and questionnaire forms. After listening to his story, I asked about his denominational standards regarding sexual behavior. He said he knew that rape and extramarital sex were not acceptable by these standards. Again he explained that what he was doing to his wife was not rape, and that the sexual encounter with her friend was innocent fun for all. He seemed shocked and angered that I would use the word rape.

I suggested that he go home and study the word rape and then come to the next appointment and tell us how this was different from what he had done with his wife and her friend. He never showed up for that appointment; his wife came alone. She seemed confused and angry. She appreciated what I had tried to do, but she was married and wanted to stay married. She was going to stay with her husband and felt she did not need any more counseling. I have since learned that they are divorced, and she is in treatment for depression.

COMMENTARY

Rape is the forceful use of another individual for sexual gratification. Clergy are normal human beings with normal needs. Abuse lies in not abiding by an appropriate standard of morality. Each distortion of human sexuality presented in these chapters produces victims, perpetrators, and consequences for persons and society. Victim, perpetrator, and consequences are not always as clear in one case as in another. Incest, for example, has a clear victim and ripples of consequence for others.

Part of the sexual revolution is the redefinition of rape. We used to think of rape as the forceful, anonymous manhandling of a woman by a man, with intercourse of some kind being perpetrated on her. This is a narrow definition of a wider phenomenon—the enforced taking of pleasure at another person's expense. Using the term rape in this wider sense may now help us understand some serious human misconceptions.

For example, it is a misconception to believe that I have the right to take anything I have the power to take. It is rape for a pastor to knowingly violate his denomination's standards, his congregation's expectations, and his ordination vows by getting sexual pleasure outside a committed relationship. The use of power and privilege and rationalizing responsibilities cannot be justified or excused in traditional or contemporary belief systems or in behavior. It may help to remind ourselves that even if we use these to gain pleasure, we do not thereby gain deep, long-term satisfaction and a sense of fulfilling our calling. Rape is a distortion of intimacy and the sacramental qualities of procreation. It violates personhood and spiritual leadership roles. It allows lust and the desire for power to corrupt human relationships.

The case study reported in this chapter depicts two of the many types of rape: marital rape and friend rape. During the early stages of the contemporary sexual revolution, another variation occurred among clergy, as it did in the general population. This was spouse-swapping, the typical form of which was for married couples who were friends to exchange spouses for sexual relations for a brief time. Males found this to be highly stimulating. Females reported some excitement, and often participated willingly, even initiating such exchanges on occasion. As they were accepting a freer expression of their own sexuality, women sometimes found this to be a relatively safe way to explore new ideas about sexuality. In retrospect, women authors and therapists call this activity another abuse by men, much as the current live-in arrangements often make women more vulnerable than men. Such relationships help us analyze the deeper meanings of rape. They help us understand how we still expect women to set the limits of sexual expression and men to be freer and more predatory. Women who accept such relationships are often deemed to be equally responsible as though no rape could occur. We are beginning to understand the sexual inequality of power, the imbalance of information and experience, the injustice of women's vulnerability to pregnancy, solo parenthood, financial loss. Consent to sexual relations with unwanted partners, then, does not eliminate the fact of rape, it demonstrates how poorly our society has understood the needs and rights of women. Studying such issues should push men to understand their responsibility for their own sexual actions and for their use of power. Sometimes such insights even lead men and women to approach each other with sensitized equality.

9

SEXUAL HARASSMENT

We have already observed sexual approaches by a pastor to his wife's friend in the previous chapter on rape. Sexual harassment is any attention—verbal, visual, or physical contact—that is unwanted by the recipient. As with rape, it is the receiver or victim who defines the attention as harassing.

AN INTERN AND HER SUPERVISING PASTOR

In our first appointment, a woman in her mid-fifties told me of her impending divorce from a clergy spouse of nearly thirty years, with whom she had five children. She had decided to go to seminary and was in her senior year, doing her internship. She was assigned to a midlife clergyman in a medium-sized church, a pastor considered quite successful. Her new mentor went out of his way to help her be happy in his parish. He and his wife entertained her and introduced her to many influential members of the congregation.

Shortly after she began her internship with him, the pastor invited her to ride with him to a regular denominational meeting. As they drove to the meeting, he was exceptionally concerned about her comfort. He stopped along the way and bought her coffee, then lunch. After the meeting he took her to a luxurious restaurant for drinks and dinner. On the way home she became sleepy, and he invited her to lay her head on his shoulder.

There were subsequent trips and many office encounters. He flattered her and encouraged her to preach and lead meetings. She began to feel indebted to him and grew to regard him affectionately as a father figure. So entranced was she by this mentor relationship that she barely resisted his hand on her thigh while driving to a meeting, or his frequent hugs in the office. She awakened to her plight only when they had sex.

Her divorce proceedings had become hostile. Her husband threatened to tell the judge of her sexual relationship with this pastor unless she yielded custody of the children. It began to dawn on her that she was being victimized, that there must be collusion between her husband and this pastor. In her anger and fear she made the appointment at our office.

After hearing her story, I asked what she believed should happen and how this would be arranged. She was not very decisive, so it took several appointments for her to talk through this whole situation and to verbalize what she felt. After several sessions she decided that her treatment by the pastor and her husband was sexual harassment. She was unable to extricate herself from her own guilt, however, until a female therapist helped her understand her vulnerable position and the seduction perpetrated upon her. Her yielding to the seduction did not make her responsible for the behavior of her husband or the pastor.

Finally the woman became focused enough to engage a lawyer of her own. This lawyer helped her end the intimidation from her husband. The pastor's seductive and demanding behavior did not stop, however, even though she begged and pleaded. In fact, her pleadings only made her more attractive to this domineering pastor. We encouraged her to choose a course of action that would be most nearly what she would be proud of in herself as a clergyperson. One afternoon I received a conference phone call from a therapist colleague. On the phone with her were the intern and her bishop. She had gathered her courage and gone to tell the bishop the story. This bishop corroborated her story with us and said he would have a meeting with this pastor very soon and straighten all this out. The woman was transferred to another parish. She continued in counseling with us until she decided she could handle her own life. Her mentor and seducer was reprimanded privately by the bishop, but he remained in his parish with no public scandal.

COMMENTARY

Sexual harassment, a relatively new concept, is one person's imposition on another of any unacceptable sexual communication or activity. Harassment can be a matter of a risqué joke or innuendo, an unacceptable glance, a personal insult, overly solicitous behavior, an unwelcome touch, hug, or kiss, attempted seduction, fondling, or intercourse. However subtle or blatant, whatever the degrees of seriousness one might attach to various words or actions, what makes it sexual harassment is that it is unacceptable to the person on the receiving end.

We in the church consider ourselves moral and caring. It is often difficult for male clergy to believe that they might be involved in sexual harassment. But they have been involved for centuries; and today, even as the gender revolution is helping women to act freely in the management of their sexuality, harassment by males continues. In fact, the sexual revolution makes some men think that they can get away with more. Let us be very clear about a crucial truth: Many women do insist that they have the right to be sexually active outside marriage, and that sex is something they have a right to enjoy, but that does not make them fair game for any man. The whole point of the gender and the sexual revolutions, in fact, is just the opposite.

I recognize that in this time of dramatic change the issues have become more complex. Men and women work side by side in many occupations, and it has become increasingly acceptable for them to be close friends. The line between teamwork and friendship can become blurred, and friendship can turn into sexual involvement. But as the case study in this chapter shows, manipulation of the situation can be the most subtle and cruel kind of harassment.

I have dealt with both heterosexual and homosexual harassment cases involving male clergy and secretaries, custodians, adult and child parishioners, and women clergy. With the increase in numbers of women clergy, there are cases of harassment by females. There are even cases of mutual harassment and of mutual seduction. All of these are equally objectionable, and the members of one sex cannot afford to condemn the abuses of the other. Most sexual harassment cases involving the clergy, however, remain the harassment of women by clergymen. The incredible variety of cases reminds us of the vulnerability of all humans and of the opportunities for abuse that go with the clergy role, whoever fills it.

Whatever the nature of the harassment, it can be painful and even devastating for the victim. A woman harassed by a pastor often feels intimidated by the inequality of power in their relationship. If he is able to threaten her job security or her reputation, she may feel that she has no option but to allow the harassment. If, on the one hand, a woman who feels powerless to stop it allows harassment to continue, the result is likely to be a strong feeling that her personhood has been deeply violated, a loss of belief in her own worth, damage to her religious faith, and despair for her future. If, on the other hand, a woman resists or fights harassment, she may pay an enormous emotional, physical, and spiritual price. She may be defined as a scolding mother-figure or accused of disloyalty, extremism, or vindictiveness. Rumors may be circulated about her, and her personal faith may be questioned. It is possible, of course, for a few women to accuse or to threaten using sexual harassment for illegitimate purposes. But my experience is that this is infrequent when compared to actual harassment incidents. I believe the victim until compelling counterevidence surfaces.

Clergy and their victims may not recognize sexual harassment; they may also deny it. The church has a responsibility in this matter. It is not demeaning to the church and the clergy to speak openly about sexual harassment in the church. It is demeaning, unjust, and damaging to everybody not to address and attack the problem. One of the clearest tasks emerging from our growing awareness of sexual harassment is the clarification, dissemination, and enforcement of codes of professional ethics for clergy, and the treatment of the causes and elimination of settings conducive to such behavior.

It is unrealistic for the church to assume that victims and perpetrators know their rights, know what is unacceptable behavior, know that investigation and discipline will be enforced, and know that appropriate therapies are available, unless this is stated clearly and authoritatively. We can and should expect good judgment in clergy. Distorted gender training, even in the church, permits sexual harassment at a conscious and unconscious level, unless it is dealt with clearly.

PART THREE

CASES IN OTHER
CLERGY SEXUAL ISSUES

10

HOMOSEXUAL ORIENTATION

This part brings together clergy sexual issues as distinct from the examples of sexual malfeasance grouped under sexual addiction. This is another way of saying that the star factor seems far less explanatory for this sundry group (except perhaps in the instance of sexual incompatibility) than for clergy sexual malfeasances. Nevertheless, I feel strongly that the church's discussion of ministry and sexuality needs to include these sexual issues.

Most homosexually oriented (and bisexually oriented) persons do not want to change their sexual orientation. Instead, they seek openness and affirmation. Gay persons themselves often do not understand their homosexuality until adulthood. Ordained homosexual clergy live in fear of discovery and rejection. Some have sought me out, and it is about the lives of these persons that I write.

LESBIANISM

Her opening statements in our first counseling appointment indicated a growing feeling of affection for a woman friend, and a feeling of dissatisfaction with her marriage. She felt confused by this development and said it was not the way she wanted to feel. She said she wanted to know why she felt this way about her friend, and why her marriage felt less satisfying. I asked her how she usually resolved such confusion. She replied that talking it out usually helped.

For several appointments she talked about her friend, who also was married. She told how their affection for each other had grown. Recently, she and her friend had fondled each other, undressed, and engaged in mutual masturbation. This had been both satisfying and confusing for her. The day after this encounter, her friend had called and said she did not want to continue their friendship.

She and her husband, a theologian and counselor, had an unusually open and mutually supportive relationship. She had told him about this encounter immediately. He was very supportive, but he was also devastated and cried with her. They decided not to tell any friends but to seek help from me. When I asked if he might join us, she said yes, but not until she had a chance to sort things out.

After several sessions, the woman wondered if she might be lesbian; but she did not like this conclusion and hoped that her sexual encounter with her friend had been happenstance. We did a sexual history and found her dating and social patterns to be typical. But then she remembered that she had felt strong erotic reactions to two women in the past, a college roommate and a more casual friend. There had been some hugs and casual, playful fondling with both of them, but no overt sexual behavior. Neither friendship had continued. She seemed surprised to recall the sexual attraction, which she had never admitted to herself or the women involved.

The pattern seemed clear; the woman was shaken. She spent one session crying profusely as she told of her guilt feelings and fear of losing the marriage. We discussed her personal faith and the theological and spiritual ramifications of sexual orientation. She was stuck between her belief that both sex outside of marriage and homosexuality were wrong and her realization that her feelings were real and strong. She also was grief stricken at the prospect of hurting or losing her husband.

At this point, the husband came for an individual session. He loved his wife and was very happy with her. The revelation of her sexual encounter saddened him, and he was convinced she was a lesbian. He was confused by all that was happening, because his theology agreed with hers.

When we resumed joint sessions, they came to the conclusion that she would give up her relationship with her woman friend, and they would continue their marriage, emphasizing communication. Both seemed relieved and content. Our counseling sessions ended.

A little over a year later, I heard in a letter that the couple had moved to another church and community. The wife had been unable to eliminate sexual feelings for her friend, and the relationship had been resumed. She said she and her husband wanted an appointment. It was obvious when they came that their attitudes had changed. This time they wanted to try keeping the marriage going and accepting her sexual relationship with her friend as part of it. They said they had changed their theology and had come to believe God's gift of sexuality did not have to conform to social norms. As we reviewed the pitfalls of such an arrangement, they remained firm in their decision and set up a strategy for regular visits between the two women, away from home and the children. Again, our sessions ended.

It was only about seven months until the phone call came, with her indication that they needed to talk again. This time they both indicated that the arrangement was too painful. They had decided now to get an amicable divorce and remain good friends, while they pursued their own relationships. They did this, and his church and their in-laws were very supportive, though pained and confused. Everyone thought they had an ideal marriage. According to my last report, this strategy continues. They remain good friends. He is planning to remarry. She is staying single while her friend decides whether or not to get a divorce and join her. At last report, both women are attending seminary.

MODIFYING BEHAVIOR

The story of another marriage reveals further aspects of homo-sexuality and intimate relationships. This dual-ordained couple's relationship demonstrates that at least in some cases, sexual orientation can be effectively modified.

Their appointments began with the woman in a rather long-term pastoral counseling relationship at our office. She knew she was gay; she came searching for ways to control her sexual feelings and expressions of them. She had been in several sexual relationships with women in her previous and present pastorates, and had no problem accepting her sexual orientation. But she said she knew it was irresponsible and dangerous to continue her pattern of sexual expression, and wished to change it.

Since she was so firmly convinced of her desire to change the expression of her sexuality, we proceeded on that course. We discussed our strategy at length and included the following: daily journaling, a healthy exercise and nutrition regimen, spiritual disciplines, a cessation of sexually intimate relationships with women (the primary one was terminated gradually, with the other woman in therapy elsewhere), a review of her sexual history, and a commitment to regular appointments at my office.

In our counseling appointments she regularly did a free-association report of her thoughts and feelings. We continually reinforced her spiritual disciplines. We developed a pattern of re-imaging her sexual fantasies. As this pattern was slowly shifted to fantasies of male partners, she agreed to resume dating males. She had a couple of good male friends; but one was married and the other was much older, so she did not consider them potential partners. At one appointment she reported meeting a male pastor; they had begun to date. That relationship developed. As it did, the two learned that each was gay and that each wanted to change this orientation. They asked if they could come to our office together to explore the possibility of marriage.

I suggested an individual appointment with him. In this appointment it was quickly apparent that he was quite knowledgeable about sexuality and pastoral counseling. He had been in intensive counseling with a seminary professor some years before; in that counseling he had confirmed his homosexuality and his intention to change it. He had done rather well in continuing his celibacy and even dating several women, though without much affection, until the present relationship.

As we resumed joint pastoral counseling, we did a typical premarital checklist and review. The man and woman indicated a sincere delight in finding a potential marriage partner who was on a similar emotional and spiritual pilgrimage. They felt little erotic attraction for each other but agreed that sexual expression would be acceptable between them.

It was nearly a year before the wedding occurred. Both of their congregations were ecstatic and shared in arranging an elaborate wedding. Then the "hard part," as they both called it, began. They had difficulty sleeping together; and though they could hug and kiss easily, sexual intercourse seemed impossible, for he was unable to sustain an erection. After several months of frustration, we discovered that his grief and loss process was incomplete. The wedding, it turned out, had been a symbolic end to a sexual identity he found difficult to lose.

They persisted in their support of each other's struggle, however, and at last report had given birth to a daughter and adopted an infant boy.

COMMENTARY

Few issues frighten the church as much as homosexuality. It is not surprising that the votes by denominational bodies on ordaining declared and practicing homosexual candidates have been resolved on conservative theological grounds. As a matter of fact, however, the church has been knowingly or unknowingly ordaining homosexual persons for centuries; and the record of homosexual pastors is at least as good as that of heterosexuals. The main practical consequences of homophobia and denominational policy are that gay, lesbian, and bisexual pastors—this last group a significant number of clergy—live an excruciating ordeal of fear, anger, and guilt regarding their sexual orientation and the attitude of the church toward it. The spouses and families of these pastors also suffer inordinately.

The time has come for honest consideration of the issues. This must involve study of the Bible in a way that goes beyond proof-texting to support or oppose homosexuality. It also must involve our growing scientific understanding of sexual development and orientation, while acknowledging that there remains much that we do not understand. It must provide standards of morality that apply equally to all persons. Most of all, it must involve rational and nonrational discernment, the use of our spiritual capacity for understanding the rhythms and purposes of God's creation, even when these seem to contradict traditional theology.

As the case studies in this chapter demonstrate, homosexual persons choose different ways of dealing with their orientation. Some set out to change it and are successful in the effort. The struggle is momentous, but for them it is worth it. A pastoral counselor, however liberal and accepting of homosexuality, must be willing to help people who have made that decision accomplish what they have set out to do or should not work with such a person. Very few homosexuals are able to change their orientation, according to recent data. They want to affirm who they are, and to do so they need the affirmation of others.

11

MASTURBATION

Masturbation is an almost universal practice. Infants typically begin erotic self-fondling at about eighteen months. Ordinarily masturbation lessens with development, but for many men and women it never totally ceases. Without providing limits and sexual alternatives, masturbation can move from an issue of sexuality to become a problem of malfeasance. Combined with fantasies and the use of pornography, it can lead to sexually inappropriate or abusive behavior. Yet I include this chapter under sexual issues because masturbation remains an option as a means of pleasure, as a coping device, and sometimes as acting-out behavior.

A YOUNG WOMAN

A relatively young, single, female pastor sought me out after I spoke at a clergy gathering on the subject of intimacy and spirituality. She said she did not have any big problems, but something had been bothering her for quite a while. Now that her schedule was more relaxed, she wanted to take time to think it through with professional assistance. In the first appointment she told of her call, training, and placement in her first church. She had been there for two years and enjoyed the clergy role.

But now that she was familiar with her activities and the town, and less distracted by newness, she was feeling more and more lonely.

"I'm with people a lot," she said, "but I need another kind of relationship. I want to be with people who will listen to me instead of me always listening to them." These comments gave us a chance to discuss the half-intimacies of the clergy role—relationships in which people feel free to share their feelings and needs with the pastor but do not allow the pastor to share needs and feelings with them. This makes the intimacy between them a one-way process, with the parishioner feeling nurtured and the pastor often feeling drained. This pastor had a number of friends from seminary and her hometown, but she did not get to see them very often. So we spent an appointment thinking of ways to strengthen her support system.

At the next appointment she said, "I know what the problem is. I still need a good relationship with a man." We reviewed her dating and sexual history. She had had a good dating history, including a close sexual relationship with a man in college. When she had told him of her call to pastoral ministry and her enrollment in seminary, he had broken the relationship, saying he could not stand the thought of being married to a pastor. This had hurt and confused her. At seminary, however, she had recovered by dating some interesting men, and by forming close, supportive relationships with several women who had endured similar experiences. Seminary work also included several helpful support groups. But in the isolated small town where she had her first pastorate, there were no individuals or groups available to her. Everyone had family, old friends, and work groups. She was welcomed as pastor, but no one seemed interested in being her friend. Without supportive friends, the yearning for a primary intimate partner had become a deep loneliness. "I dread going home to that empty house some nights," she said.

Then the story came together. Memories of her former lover had began to fill her mind; she had got into the habit of thinking of him and having long masturbation sessions on her lonely evenings. This relieved some of her empty feelings, but she found herself getting depressed. She disliked masturbation, even though it was pleasurable. It reminded her of how alone she was, yet relieved the pain of loneliness enough so that she did not feel compelled to look for a social life and appropriate male companions. She felt stuck with an unsatisfactory sexual pattern.

Her depression, fortunately, had not yet sapped her enthusiasm for life or for creative change. After assessing her situation, she decided to develop a closer friendship with a nearby woman pastor in similar circumstances. They decided to become a team and develop social activities. They coordinated their schedules and began to put their free days together so they could drive to the city and stay overnight. They found some women friends in an exercise group at the YWCA, and they met several men in a bicycle club. At our last appointment she was speaking with excitement about one particular man; masturbation and loneliness, she said, were no longer a problem.

A MIDDLE-AGED MAN

A middle-aged pastor presented a different problem. In our second appointment he spoke of the great guilt he felt about his habit of masturbating. It was quickly apparent in our counseling sessions that this pastor was a workaholic. His work patterns had been successful, for he was widely regarded as an effective pastor; but the stress he generated with his intense schedule seemed to be relieved most quickly through masturbation. He had a long history of this behavior. In his youth he had worried about masturbation, because he had heard all the typical myths about the damage it does. He also had worried about the religious and moral aspects of it. But over the years he had rationalized this way of reducing stress and settled into a habitual pattern. After tense church meetings and stressful days, he found regular relaxation through masturbating with pornographic literature.

His sexual relationship with his wife had deteriorated into an occasional lovemaking episode. She had asked him many times for more intimacy, but he had a ready excuse in his schedule pressures. As his affection for his wife waned, he found it more exciting and pleasurable to fantasize seductive relationships. This appeared to be the source of his guilt. He felt badly about depriving his wife of the pleasure of sexual intimacy; he felt guilty about using pornographic literature. These did not fit his expectations of a spiritually alive and active pastor. But he now felt nearly helpless to break the pattern. Since he had tried New Year's resolutions, promises to God, and great efforts of will, we agreed to ask his wife for assistance. She responded positively.

In the first visit in which she participated, she cried with relief when he told her his problem. She had assumed for years that he was having an affair. She also had been giving some thought to what it was going to be like to grow old married to a man from whom she received little affection. Obviously, the timing was right for them to make a change. They began to reserve one night a week for intimate and playful times together. Aware that his behavior would not change overnight, she agreed that he could masturbate any time he wanted, except on their night out. Their relationship quickly improved as they both invested in it enthusiastically, and at our last appointment he indicated much less urge to masturbate.

COMMENTARY

The current terminology calls it monosex, solo sex, self-sex, autosex, or self-pleasuring. The changing terms reflect changing attitudes. Masturbation has not changed as a process but it is now practiced, discussed, and researched with less disapproval. For many it is an accepted part of normal sexual experience.

Masturbation is included in these chapters on clergy sexual issues even though for many clergy it becomes a problem. For some it produces mental anguish and guilt, for others occasional anxiety. For some it has become an addiction. Masturbation becomes problematic when used as a stress reducer or as a substitute for intimacy.

Monosex is intensely private, as its name implies. But research on sexual practices indicates relatively few people now believe masturbation is evil. Many people do it. In fact, it appears to be in itself a relatively harmless alternative to manipulative or promiscuous intimacy. Until this generation, masturbation was almost exclusively a male phenomenon. Gender programming, gender modeling, and stimulation in the media, along with differences in biochemistry, disposed boys more than girls to discover and practice monosex. Recent surveys show that women are catching up. In fact, clinical literature and books can now be found that encourage and guide women in sexual self-discovery.

As indicated in the first case, monosex as a substitute for intimacy with another can become a stopgap. It can be pleasurable and reassuring, and it can relieve us of sexual vulnerabilities. But it also reminds us of our loneliness, it distracts us from the need to seek more satisfying forms of intimacy, and it can engender guilt and loss of self-esteem if it is believed to be sinful.

In my experience with clergy, the use of masturbation as a stress reducer as in the second case is problematic. Since stress (high-intensity stimulation) is increasingly a part of our lives, any method found useful in reducing the unpleasantness of stress will likely become more and more common. The use of alcohol, drugs, food, sleep, sex, and so forth as stress reducers means their use will likely become habitual, perhaps even addictive. The addictive danger appears most likely for the person of low self-esteem who finds the sexual fantasies reassuring, and for the high-intensity worker (workaholic) whose life revolves around compulsive polarities such as work and collapse, passion and apathy. When the stress peaks, the stress reducer must be employed. The cycle repeats itself habitually and is cued by familiar symbols.

The resolution for both of these pastors was positive for several reasons. Both had sound egos and a self-generated desire to

change the behavior. Neither was suffering from excessive turmoil about the sinfulness of masturbation. Both had developed
good personal support systems, and both found a professional
counseling process compatible with their needs. Simply trying
to change a stress-reduction habit by fiat, because of guilt, is
unlikely to be successful.

12

SEXUAL INCOMPATIBILITY

Marriage research indicates that unreal expectations, poor models, lack of support systems, infidelity, career conflicts, and money problems cause many conflicts in marriages. Incompatibility—personality differences that sabotage intimacy—is often at the core of these sources of conflict. The clergy I have worked with—a self-selected sample—were seriously considering divorce at a rate four times greater than their state's clergy divorce rate; twice as many actually had been divorced as compared to that rate. Pastors without healthy primary intimate relationships are more vulnerable to burnout, incompetence, and moral malfeasance than those with such relationships.

CHANGED EXPECTATIONS

An effusive female voice on the phone told me how she had admired my work and was so anxious to bring her husband in so I could "get him straightened out." After listening to a few more flattering comments, I was able to get an appointment time set.

She swept into the office, nodded to our secretary, and fixed her dark eyes on me. When she was sure she had my attention, she widened her eyes, then slowly let her face become a glowing smile. With a dramatic swish of her long skirt, she came over to me and took my hand in both of hers. Then her carefully made-up face took on a sincere and serious look as she said, "Oh, Dr. Rediger, you don't know how long I've waited for this appointment. I'm so thankful that you found time to see us!"

The yellow warning lights were flashing in my head as I welcomed her; then I turned to her tall, lean husband and introduced myself. He looked a bit bored but wary as he acknowledged my greeting. I ushered them into my office. She passed very close to me and carefully gave me the glowing smile again. Then she elegantly reclined in one of our comfortable chairs, waited until I looked from him to her, and dramatically crossed her long legs.

I went through the brief explanation of our service and then asked what they wanted to accomplish. She widened her eyes again, and said, "Oh, Dr. Rediger, you won't believe the things I'm about to tell you!" Then for about half an hour she told me explicit details of the kind of sexual activities her husband demanded of her. "Why, he often asks me to go along on his driving trips to clergy meetings," she said. "And he always makes me do oral sex on him while he's driving! Can you imagine such behavior from a minister?"

The wife then regaled us with titillating details of the lingerie her husband forced her to buy, the way he often posed her in the nude and took pictures of her, the way he frequently joined her in the shower, and the many different positions he placed her in for intercourse. When she became aware that my matter-of-fact attitude was not going to change, she began to modify her performance. Then she said, "I really don't mind sex, and I do try to be a dutiful wife, but you have to make my husband realize that I won't submit to this unchristian behavior any more. I will give him sex, if he will be decent about it. But I'm not going to let him turn me into a strumpet, even if I have to divorce him!" She settled back in the chair, crossed her arms, lowered her eyes, and was silent.

After a few moments her husband began to speak in a rather

loud voice. "I feel I must set the record straight here," he said. "Some of what my wife says is true, but there's another side to it. I'm very much male, and I'm not ashamed of it. And my wife is very attractive. What's wrong with my wanting to have some excitement with her? But I do get rather angry at her constant criticism of my sexual behavior with her. She seems to object to everything I want sexually. And I'm getting a little tired of always doing the initiating, and always listening to her objections. But I do have to admit that she seldom refuses. She just objects a lot, and accuses me of being an animal instead of a minister of the gospel."

"Tell me how you two met," I asked.

"How we met? What's that got to do with our problem?" he responded.

"Well," I replied, "your reports of your relationship sound so clear, it must have been this way for a long time."

"I'll tell you how we met," she said brightly. "He was a minor league ballplayer and I was in my first year as a teacher. Another teacher and I decided to go to a ballgame. We each picked out a guy on the home team to try to meet. After the game, our guys came out of the locker room together, and we introduced ourselves. They invited us to a nearby bar. We liked each other and went together for several months.

"Boy, those were hot times," she recalled with a roll of her eyes. "We had great sex for about a year. Then we got converted, would you believe? My husband felt called to be a pastor, went to seminary, and has served three churches now. There was a big change in our lives, and ever since then our marriage has been more and more unhappy. I can't figure out why."

Her curiosity about why what was once so good was now experienced as bad gave the needed opening. I asked, "If you do the same things now that you did before conversion and pastoral ministry, and enjoyed them so much then and find them so painful now, what could be the cause of the change from pleasure to pain?"

She replied, "Well, you ought to know that! Abnormal sex is

sinful, especially for pastors. I'm the only one trying to keep the sex in this marriage normal." There was a long silence. Each was apparently thinking very hard. They were trying on some new insights. He turned to her and said, "You really believe that, don't you?" "Well, of course," she said. "Isn't that what Christianity is about? Isn't that what you've been preaching all these years?"

I suggested then that before our next appointment they read the first three chapters of Genesis and talk with each other about the goodness of God's creation. They returned with a glowing report. They had verified the positiveness of their sexuality and rediscovered the pleasure of sexual intimacy. The change was apparent in her shedding the seductive mask and in his relaxed and loving behavior. Both told of the relief they felt as they united their energies in satisfying sexual intimacy and the joy of the ministry they shared.

This example of self-imposed incompatibility reminds us that some conflicts in marriage and intimate sexuality are the products of mistaken ideas and training—even of distorted theology. There was actually a compatible relationship underneath the imposed distortion. Not all incompatibilities are only apparent, of course. Yet even some imposed ones do not yield as quickly to corrections. What this case demonstrates is the power of our minds and ideas to distort the freedom and joy of God's creation and of pastoral ministry.

BASIC PERSONALITY CONFLICT

Let us consider a case in which the incompatibility is more primary and real. This couple was very young and relatively new to pastoral ministry. They had one young child, born as he was graduating from seminary and as she was completing her master's degree in social work. They had been in his first parish for about three years. He was doing well as a pastor, but she could not find work in her profession.

In their first appointment at our office, she complained about feeling at loose ends and about his constant criticism of her aimlessness, poor housekeeping, and indifference to parenting and his church work. He complained about her irritability, sexual aloofness, and disregard for his work. For three appointments they continued this pattern of complaining, identifying the absence of sexual affection as a key indicator of the general malaise.

During the fourth appointment I asked each of them to draw some representation of their marital relationship. He carefully listed two columns of complaints—one for each of them. Then she turned his sheet aside and quickly sketched a skillful and colorful drawing of a man and woman side by side. The man was big and straight and dressed in clerical garb. The woman, portrayed in vivid colors, was very small by comparison, with her hair, arms, and legs askew.

The dramatic differences in their portrayals of the marriage provided discussion material for two appointments. Then I gave them the Myers-Briggs personality-type indicator. At the next appointment we discussed their distinct differences in personality characteristics. This inventory helps persons understand their own and each other's distinct characteristics, without judging any of them as good or bad; and it helps persons understand likely effects of putting two personality types together in an intimate relationship.

This couple found the device very enlightening. Then as they read and discussed Jacquelyn Wonder and Priscilla Donovan's *Whole Brain Thinking*, they began to understand the significant implications of split-brain theory for human relationships. The differences between a person whose perspective is dominated by the left hemisphere of the brain and that of one dominated by the right brain can be dramatic. Left-brain dominants tend to be structured and thought oriented, while right-brain dominants tend to be spontaneous and feeling oriented. Both think their perspective is accurate and exclusive of the other perspective, unless they have learned to "lateralize"—use and appreciate both sides of the brain.

It was clear that one spouse in this clergy couple was an "artist" (right brain) and one was a "technician" (left brain). As we discussed this, I learned that she had an undergraduate degree in theater and arts. She had gotten into social work because her best friend did it, and because she could not see much use for her arts degree in her life with a pastor. He, by contrast, had always had a plan for his life and conducted his ministry in a very orderly fashion. These two fine people were well on their way to becoming enemies without knowing why until they began to understand their differences and explore ways to blend their perspectives into teamwork.

Real incompatibility involves such distinct differences. The differences are basic, not the result of wrong ideas or poor training; they are not likely to change significantly over a lifetime. In fact, these individual characteristics must be used, appreciated, and affirmed, by ourselves first and then by those close to us. Without such affirmation it is likely that there will be conflict, resentments, and despair. But when unique individual characteristics are appreciated by a couple, they can teach and support each other, divide responsibilities realistically, and love the half of themselves that the other person mirrors.

This couple had not yet let their relationship harden into disrespect and efforts to change each other. So they found excitement and growth as we explored possibilities for their teamwork and for their sexual relationship. As with the first case, sexual relations were symptoms of an underlying divergence.

COMMENTARY

We can smile at those who call any disagreement in marriage or intimate relationships incompatibility. But frequently there is serious disharmony in primary intimate relationships, and consequently a great deal of pain and dysfunction. A clergyperson without a well-functioning primary intimate relationship is likely to be less effective in pastoring and more vulnerable to burnout, malfeasance, and addictions than one who has this support.

Sex is not the whole of intimacy, but when sexual relationships are not satisfying, there is a tendency to imagine that all is lost. My experience with clergy indicates that sexual incompatibility is a common problem. In the past it was typically denied, ignored, or accepted as part of life. Now either spouse (or both) is more likely to see it as a significant problem and demand a remedy, seek divorce, or find sexual liaisons outside marriage.

There are various sexual incompatibilities, of course, from timing to favored positions to frequency to motivations. I want to focus on the ones that are most frequent for clergy couples and those most specific to the clergy role.

A basic cause of incompatibility is gender programming. Generally speaking, gender programming refers to the training and expectations given to boys and girls in the socialization process. Girls have been given dolls and piano lessons and taught how to be female, while boys have been given toy trucks and footballs and taught how to be male. Given the recent gender revolution, many of us tend to think we are more liberated from these gender stereotypes than we are. We may then make the mistake of expecting a spouse to be more free from gender programming than he or she is, of expecting a spouse to perform according to traditional gender roles, or of confusing our own behavior with freedom when it is actually shaped by our gender role.

There is nothing wrong with traditional gender roles as long as they fit the two individuals' personality types and the couple's shared expectations. Many marriages are still happily based upon the tradition of "women's work" and "men's work." But the ideal for marriage has shifted from gender role performance to intimacy with equality. Even though this sounds like a good idea to many, we are poorly equipped to handle it. Our habits, expectations, job markets, and social approval patterns are still oriented more toward traditional gender roles than toward intimate equality.

It is still very difficult for a woman to break out of the submissive-supportive role in a marriage without becoming angry or having strong new models and support. It is very difficult for men to share control and to cultivate their gentler characteristics without confusion and fear, and without having gentle new models and support. The best context for rethinking gender roles and determining the type of relationship wanted is a marriage in which both partners understand and appreciate themselves and each other, and in which both are willing to negotiate differences and explore new options. But it will likely take several generations to clarify options, build supportive models, and find compatibility in intimate equality.

The church can be an appropriate context for exploring significant changes, and clergy couples can be valuable models. But it is obvious that churches and clergy are human, with all the limitations that accompany our humanity. Fortunately, the strengths and spiritual resources of church and clergy are also available for growing in grace and the building of loving relationships.

13

SEXUAL TORMENT

Sex researchers confirm that males often fantasize about sex and have self-conscious reactions to this fantasizing. As women are freed from gender taboos, their sexual fantasies are increasing. Adults who were brought up in rigid, narrow, and judgmental environments tend to suffer from sexual torment—excessive, persistent guilt about their sexual feelings and behavior. This condition should be recognized as a debilitating emotional and spiritual malady that requires competent treatment.

A GUILT-RIDDEN PASTOR

A pastor in his late thirties came to me for pastoral counseling and immediately challenged, "I'm tired of this self-torture. I want to see if you can relieve me of the burden of my sexual guilt!" As we explored the patterns of his sexual history, it became clear that one focusing experience distorted his sexual perceptions and behavior. When he was in the fifth grade he sneaked into his parents' bedroom one day, took a pair of his mother's panties, and masturbated with them. The experience was intensely pleasurable, but it left a crippling experience of shame and guilt. After that act, sex for him was not a normal dimension of his life; it was the rape of his mother. Whenever he felt sexual attraction and desire, these normal human experiences triggered the torment of that eleven-year-old's experience, plus all the compulsive fascination and the accumulated guilt of feelings experienced later in life.

A metaphor came to mind as I listened to this pastor describe his life at age eleven. "It sounds to me," I said, "like loading down your first bicycle with heavy bags of garbage and then trying to enjoy it!" He was silent for a while. Then he slowly smiled, nodded his head, and told me of his first bike. It was the pride of his life, for he had saved his paper-route money for two years to buy it—a little while before this masturbation incident. After the incident, it had been difficult for him to enjoy it. The metaphor, obviously, was apt for his experience.

After several months of counseling, the pastor decided to tell his wife about his sexual torment. Listening to his story and feelings, she expressed her confusion. She was able to acknowledge his experience and relate one of her own: Early in life when her father picked her up and hugged her, she would wrap her arms and legs around him. On one occasion, the pressure of his big belt buckle stimulated her clitoris. It was a wonderful feeling. After that, she made it a practice for years to run enthusiastically to her father when he came home and leap into his arms, embracing him with arms and legs, hoping for, and sometimes achieving, a repetition of that experience. As she grew older, she acquired guilt about sex; so she began to worry about what she was doing. But she kept doing it, even through her high school years.

Though her sexual torment was not as traumatic as her husband's, she was able to relate to his torment because of her own. She finally felt released emotionally from her childhood and her parents by telling this experience to her husband. Their bond of intimacy increased as they shared their torments and experienced release from them together.

COMMENTARY

Sexual torment, especially the male experience of it, is one of the most common sexual issues among clergy. This is an inheritance from the church, prior to becoming more enlightened in its theology and preaching. Earlier, sex was allegedly considered good and necessary for human life; but almost every one of the ways it could be experienced was characterized as somehow tainted, if not as evil.

For example, I still remember how the traveling evangelists who came to town when I was a boy would set aside one evening of their revivals to talk about sex. I dreaded such sermons, yet looked forward to them with irresistible fascination. Along with the warnings of sin and threats of divine wrath, the preacher would offer illustrations of evil that set my fantasies on fire. After the sermon, my mind would race for days with thoughts of things to do with the girls in town; then I would be overwhelmed by excruciating guilt, fear, and shame. I would always end by promising God that in return for forgiveness, I would never think another sexual thought.

Seeing sexuality as a gift of God, as part of the good order of creation, and understanding many forms of sexual experience as good in themselves, not merely as tolerable within the context of conceiving a child in marriage, set me free from this torment. Yes, the gift can be abused. Sexual experience can become manipulative, abusive, addictive. But no person should have to feel tormented because he or she has felt or done something within the wide range of normal human experience at some stage of life.

Yet, some people enter the clergy role burdened by immense weight from the past. Perhaps such torment can help them to feel the pain of others. But for their sakes as well as for the good of those with whom they work, these clergy also need to know that they are God's good creation, loved by God as they really are, and that the God who loves them has been with them even as they have worked through the meaning of their sexuality. The sexual torment in the private lives of many clergy is no longer necessary.

14

TRANSVESTISM

American transvestites are almost always male and seldom homosexual. At the center of their condition is fetishism—the need to use objects that stimulate sexual arousal and orgasm. The typical transvestite is insecure in his sexual identity, secretive, moody, taciturn, and distrustful. He is also compulsive in his behavior and extremely reluctant to change it. The spouse is usually confused and resentful.

A PASTOR'S SECRET LIFE

A pastor arrived for an appointment accompanied by his wife. The man was big physically and his bearing was commanding, even intimidating. But he was friendly and immediately responsive.

He stated his case matter-of-factly. For years he had practiced cross-dressing. He particularly liked to dress in women's silky undergarments and pantyhose, and he nearly always did this before sex with his wife. Only when he did this was he able to enjoy orgasm. But he was wondering if he could rid himself of the transvestism.

When he finished, I asked his wife why she had come. She said that she also would like these practices to cease. He had done this cross-dressing without her knowledge for years, and he had told her about it only a year ago. She was shocked, hurt, and disgusted at first, she reported, but had come to accept it, somewhat reluctantly. In fact, she had come to accept his doing it in her presence before intercourse, and even helped him dress in her undergarments on occasion.

It became apparent that they had a good, intimate relationship. The future of their marriage did not depend upon his ending the transvestism, though both wanted this. I suggested taking a sexual history from both of them, and they agreed to do this in each other's presence.

Their sexual histories contained no dramatic experiences. His relationship to his parents, however, contained some of the classic sexual material associated with transvestism and some other sexual disorders—a distant relationship with his father, a very close relationship with his mother, and emotional distance between his parents. His mother was seductive. When they were in the house alone, she would sometimes bathe with the bathroom door open. Occasionally she would give him an armload of her undergarments and ask him to launder them. They never had any physical, sexual contact, but there was an erotic attachment neither of them talked about.

Both pastor and spouse had been in counseling on other occasions. They were alert to the issues, so we discussed strategies. It was apparent that both wanted change, but there appeared to be no urgent motivation for change. Their relationship was good, both were satisfied in their careers, and there appeared to be little danger of discovery or scandal. When I commented on this, he calmly indicated that he had a strong will and was accustomed to disciplining himself rigorously. She shed some tears at this time and said she really hoped they could achieve a normal marriage.

We decided on a fourfold strategy. First, he would practice imagining his cross-dressing ritual without actually doing it, and then see if their lovemaking could be satisfying. Along with this, they agreed to increase their foreplay. This was to include enjoying sensual things together (music, food, wine, fragrances, and so forth) prior to intercourse. They agreed to shower together and do full body massages several times a week, whether or not this led to intercourse. They did this for several months and found that he was unable to sustain an erection most of the time. Still, they felt some progress was being achieved.

Second, we decided that he needed to work again on his relationship to his parents. His mother had died, and his father was mentally disabled in a nursing home, so he wrote daily letters to each parent. For several weeks the pastor reviewed childhood memories, vented deep boyhood fear and anger, and then told his parents what he wanted to happen between them. The letters released some inner tensions, and there was some lessening of the pastor's cross-dressing.

Third, although we had discussed the theological, ethical, and spiritual dimensions of this situation during our appointments, we had not emphasized them. At this point, however, I felt that his spirituality could become a valuable and basic resource in resolving the conflict. We took some time to explore meditative-devotional exercises, and drew up a schedule for establishing them in daily practice. The relaxation, reassurance, and dependability of these exercises further improved the situation.

Finally, we decided that one of the reinforcing elements of the old pattern was the familiarity of ritual. The couple exchanged bedrooms with one of their children. They redecorated and arranged the room in ways that were relaxing and sensuous. They also experimented with some different ways of foreplay and intercourse. It took a number of months to break some of the old patterns and establish a new style of physical intimacy, but they reported success in achieving a much happier relationship.

COMMENTARY

There is much misinformation about transvestism in society and in the church. The mythology about this disorder promotes a sense of repulsion. Transvestites are commonly believed to be perverted, sinister voyeurs who molest children and who dress in women's clothing to gain attention. Often the public assumes that female impersonators and transsexuals (surgically changed from one sexual anatomy to the other) are transvestites, and that they became this way by being reared in an all-female household or in one where parents wanted the boy to be a girl.

The truth is, as far as we know it, that "transvestite" is a label for a rather normal man who needs to dress in women's clothing to experience full arousal and orgasm. He is almost always male, heterosexual, married, and an adequate father. He functions well except for the male role in heterosexual loving. He can have intercourse and can satisfy his spouse if she can accept his need for intimate female clothing as part of the sex act. Typically this is too painful or unacceptable to her, and she eventually leaves, becomes a nonparticipant in sex, or becomes depressed. This man usually feels intense guilt, shame, and fear about his disorder. He is typically caught in an emotional bind, for he wishes he could change (or that society would accept his needs), and yet he is unwilling to give up his transvestism for fear of never being able to enjoy sex again. Most therapists, therefore, concentrate on trying to relieve the anxieties of the transvestite so that a better balance of emotions can be achieved in his life.

Though the estimate of one million transvestites in America seems relatively small, the practice is well established. Some clergy are transvestites. My experience indicates that the transvestite pastor will be as competent, friendly, caring, and dedicated to ministry as the nontransvestite.

As the case study presented in this chapter indicates, the pastoral counseling method of choice is to reduce anxiety, offer ways to change if they are desired, and give the spouse every support technique appropriate to her needs. The marriage may have to exist with some distortions, as many marriages do. But reassurance, support, and guidance can aid the person who is a transvestite and his marriage partner to have a satisfying life and ministry. A large measure of the problem is the social unacceptance of this condition.

Successful treatment of transvestism as a psychosexual disorder requires that the person have a relatively stable situation in life, a support system, and a strong ego. These were present in the case described here. Without these the chances of changing most psychosexual disorders are considerably less. These persons also had and nurtured a religious faith that pastoral counseling enhanced.

PART FOUR

CARE FOR
CLERGY SEXUALITY

15

GUIDES TO A CLERGY SEXUAL ETHIC

The subject of professional ethics is currently receiving widespread attention. Clergy, as I have said repeatedly, need self- and group-control mechanisms. It cannot be assumed that being a member of the clergy automatically makes a person moral or capable of abiding by self-imposed limits. In this chapter I will offer some guides for the clarification of clergy sexual ethics.

CONTEXT

Clergy are the identified leaders of our society's chief moral valuing institution, the church. As such they are expected to blend several functions and to please all constituencies while providing moral leadership. This expectation can be a great burden, especially for clergy who do not have a keen sense of reality or the tools and strength to practice self-management.

Unfortunately, most clergy have been prepared for moral leadership through the academic model, which is quite limited in its understanding of human experience and everyday life. Furthermore, that model sounds to many students like the pluralism of contemporary culture. From their study of ethics, for example, seminary students often get the message that there are no absolutes and conclude that each may do what is right in his or her own mind. When they complete their training, clergy are sent out into an intense, fast-paced world that is caught up in the gender and sexual revolutions. It is a world in which the breakdown of traditional support systems invites dependence on stress reducers, one of which is sexual activity. Clergy are expected to function in this world as loners—with little attention to their own intimacy, little direct accountability, and extensive exposure to human needs and appetites. As the congregations' stars, they are highly vulnerable to pitfalls.

Human history is filled with the tension between pragmatism and absolutism—perspectives in which the world is viewed either as a functional process of factors, some of which work and some of which do not, or an idealistic world of absolute truth and standards. Ethics for the contemporary world of interdependent cultures needs a resolution of both. We also need a synthesis of the mundane and the transcendent—that which is workable within present limitations and that which calls humankind toward something greater than the self. Such a synthesis demands new ways of understanding life.

FACTORS IN SEXUALITY

Before I devise an outline of clergy sexual ethics, let me note some factors that might inform it.

Sexuality is a normal identifying aspect of our humanity. Genital function is a part of sexuality. Individual sexuality is a yearning for union with another living being, such that procreation occurs—satisfaction and new life are generated through the union. The ultimate union is with the Life Force—God. There are two basic kinds of attraction between intimate partners: biochemical attraction and the more long-term personal attraction of investment in a relationship. The best relationships appear to involve a combination of these factors and includes obligations and responsibilities. Indeed, intimacy needs to have these parts properly interrelated.

OUTLINE OF A PROFESSIONAL ETHIC

My own outline for a clergy professional ethic is structured after the Ten Commandments.

1. Love God with body, mind, and spirit.
2. Express this love toward self, others, and all creation, in a spirit of thankfulness and with conduct appropriate to a spiritual leader.
3. Discipline yourself to express caring in every thought, word, and act.
4. Learn the language of love that is unique to each creature, person, and ecological system, so that your intention to care may be perceived by them as caring.
5. Model caring on a professional level with skill and wisdom so that others may experience your integrity and be drawn toward emulating God's caring for us all.
6. Do not violate another person's body, mind, or spirit, and do not participate in the oppression of any person, community of persons, or any ecological system, and do not misuse faith and the resources entrusted to you.
7. Do not abuse your own body, mind, or spirit.
8. Do not seek your own comfort, pleasure, or aggrandizement until you understand the effects on other persons and systems.
9. Do not neglect playfulness, humor, and rest, for yourself and for other persons and systems. The joy of living and ministry is for all.
10. Before any action, think of how it will appear in a court of law, in the view of clergy peers, and in the sight of God.

These principles are reminders of the sacred trust of our call and commitment to pastoral ministry. They should be understood in conjunction with our personal religious faith. They should remind us of ministry standards mandated by our denomination's discipline.

PRACTICAL GUIDELINES

There are guidelines that can help clergy avoid legal difficulties. Most of these are well known, but we need to remind ourselves of them periodically, and to act on them lest the story we read on the front page of the local newspaper be ours.

1. When engaged in person-to-person communication (counseling, calling, planning, and so forth), avoid physical and suggestive contact; take a partner on house calls, or tell someone where you will be and for how long; have a clear, official agreement with an authoritative church board regarding counseling and individual contacts; and make use of reputable referral resources in problem situations. Be careful what you put in writing. Learn the obvious and subtle danger signals, in yourself and others, whenever there will be contact in vulnerable situations.

2. When dealing with children and troubled adults, it is wise to avoid giving advice or doing things for them that could be misinterpreted. Get parents, relatives, friends, or professionals to share responsibility for your contacts whenever possible.

3. Be as visible and caring as possible. Secrecy and unexplained private events can be dangerous.

4. Build professional and dependable contacts with local lawyers, physicians, financial consultants, and so forth. Associations with reputable persons tend to generate confidence in a pastor, as well as providing referral services.

5. Learn your denomination's code of ethics for clergy and abide by it. It is surprising how little attention is paid to formal professional ethics by denominations, clergy groups, and individual clergy. We who purport to be, or are expected to be, leaders in morality and ethics should demonstrate clearer definition of and attention to our professional behavior. Rules may seem to be impractical and subject to abuse, but the reverse is true for paying little heed to ethics. We have a believable protection in most cases when we

abide by an official code of ethics and know what "standard practices" mean for our behavior.

6. In shared responsibility settings, it is wise to have clear agreements, job descriptions, communication, and periodic evaluations. Those with whom we work closely can contribute to our vulnerability or our protection.

7. Keep yourself thinking clearly, for most entangling mistakes occur when a pastor is physically, emotionally, or spiritually unprepared to see situations clearly and manage himself or herself accordingly.

8. Keep your intimate relationships nurtured and positive. It takes a lot of energy to keep relating to people as they are. We are prepared for such relationships by keeping the ones on which we depend in good shape so they sustain us.

16

PREVENTION AND SUPPORT

In order to work creatively in the general state of things, church leaders need to understand the conditions that produced it, establish procedures for dealing with problems as they arise, and develop both short-term and long-term strategies for prevention of sexual malfeasance and growth toward moral integrity.

UNDERSTANDING THE CONTEXT

Many things contribute to clergy sexual malfeasance, of course. In my judgment the most significant are the changes in the clergy role in church and society. The life of a clergyperson is so closely identified with the role that, when it changes significantly, she or he is likely to feel confused, angry, and afraid, as well as excited and adventurous. But without the traditional role to guide and limit behavior, clergy often flounder in the new undefined freedom, even while they appear to be carrying out traditional duties in normal ways.

While we cannot foresee how the clergy role will change in the future, it will undoubtedly retain elements of the past and incorporate new behavior and rituals. Let us identify some of the contemporary dynamics and pressures affecting the clergy role and opening it up to moral malfeasance.

First, the pedestal or halo effect is nearly gone. Along with physicians, teachers, and many other professionals, clergy are more and more seen as human beings first and "experts" second. Few people now believe that clergy are closer to God than laypersons. Clergy pronouncements are now judged or ignored more often than believed, although the ancient mysteries of religion still color the clergy image in some minds. What has remained of the traditional clergy role is its stature as a moral model. We still expect clergy to have more moral integrity than laity. This pushes clergy to hide their humanness.

Second, the self-image of clergy is changing. Clergy tend more to think of themselves as normal human beings. They often live in quiet intimidation from the power brokers of the congregation and community. This rather sudden loss of status and power causes some clergy to seek control through manipulation and reassurance in sexual fantasies and gratification.

The clergy's self-image is also changing as women and men become less willing to be bound by the traditional gender roles. Women are gaining power in traditionally male-dominated institutions, which upsets many of the dependable patterns in the church. Without the traditional roles and guidelines, pastors tend to be more anxious, confused, and compulsive about expectations and reality. The sexual revolution, a factor in the larger gender revolution, has eroded much of the fear and social disapproval once associated with anything but traditional moral behavior. Pastors are expected to officiate at weddings of couples already living together. They may come to believe that if non-committed sex is acceptable for others, it is acceptable for them. The only control seems to be fear of AIDS.

Intimacy as the goal of marriage is relatively new in human history. We do not know how to produce consistent emotional closeness, for we grew up in a world based upon gender roles rather than intimacy. Now that most of us expect intimacy, we find ourselves unable to shed gender-related expectations. Men, particularly, have difficulty in understanding the dynamics of intimacy. Women, typically, allow themselves to be more dependent than intimacy warrants. Clergy, who must function often in intimate situations, are succumbing increasingly to the vulnerabilities produced by gender confusions.

Third, clergy tend to operate on the periphery of society now rather than at its center. Social policymakers used to listen to and consult clergy. Now clergy are seldom consulted, unless the clergyperson represents a significant constituency. Ethical issues tend to be resolved on scientific, medical, and political grounds rather than on theological ones. The rise of psychotherapy and counseling has decreased the perceived need for clergy. Pluralism has made the local pastor only one voice among many ideological spokespersons. The acceptance of the business model for operating the local church has reduced much of the pastor's role to that of a bureaucrat or program director.

As a result, it has become common for clergy to function as paramours—illicit lovers. Their lives are filled with pseudo-intimacies in which parishioners are open to clergy, but clergy cover their inner needs. In fact, the traditional understanding of ordination as setting apart seems to imply this. As long as there was a wife at home, or a religious community that acted as family, this model functioned well. But now clergy spouses have their own agendas and religious communities are less cohesive, making this model painfully lonely. Only the well-managed and those who fear repercussions can survive this vulnerability.

Finally, trustworthy theology, personal religious faith, and a sense of being called to pastoral ministry have long been the foundation of the clergy role. For more than a few, all of these are less compelling today than in other times. The variety and relativity of identifiable theological systems have cracked the foundation undergirding moral living; the absence of clear and specific codes of ethics for clergy essentially leaves a vacuum in standards for behavior. This often produces a laissez-faire attitude in denominational offices and a fly-by-the-seat-of-your-pants attitude among clergy. Such casualness about theology and ethics is a fragile bulwark against moral malfeasance.

MANAGING SCANDAL

Though the church has had its malfeasant clergy for centuries, contemporary conditions require new guidelines for managing both the malfeasance and the public scandal associated with it. Controlling such malfeasance and scandal is no longer a realistic option. It is likely that clergy malfeasance will continue, for the context we have discussed continues. But managing such situations, often called "damage control," is possible, and can become healing and generative.

Presently there are sporadic and uncoordinated attempts to control clergy malfeasance. The general public is becoming outspokenly intolerant, and the secular courts are more willing to accept litigation against clergy and religious organizations. Church professionals prefer to manage these situations from within. But our track record so far is not good, and victims, courts, and the public are impatient. If we wish to have the responsibility for correcting this tragic condition, we must demonstrate integrity to the public and sensitive caring to victims, congregations, and perpetrators. It is heartening to see some responsible denominational leaders moving in this direction.

Each denomination and congregation has its own policies and dynamics; no one formula for scandal management applies to every situation. But out of the devastating pain and confusion some generic guidelines have emerged that have been valuable so far.

1. Get the facts straight. We cannot always wait for all the facts, but we must have reasonable evidence that malfeasance has occurred. If we wait too long, victims suffer and perpetrators are emboldened. We also miss early opportunities to use modest interventions. On the other hand, ill-advised interventions can irreparably damage reputations and ministries.

2. Have a responsible and authorized denominational official in charge of the situation: to speak with authority and sensitivity; to guide the congregation; to remove the alleged

perpetrator from the scene; and to unify management. In some denominations the congregation has highest authority and thus should produce the authorized leader. We must remember that until there is a legitimate trial or uncoerced confession, conclusions of guilt and penalties are not appropriate. But separation of the alleged perpetrator and victim is mandatory.

3. Assess and minister to hurts and needs of involved persons. Protect and nurture all victims, primary and secondary. Inform the congregation and related persons of official actions. If the situation and official actions are not to be made public, an official designation of persons who need to know should be made. Such persons should be informed of necessary data and covenanted to confidentiality.

4. Establish limits, treatment, and reinstatement or termination options for the alleged perpetrator and any accomplices.

5. Check legal procedures and ramifications.

6. Assess damage control and related needs in the congregation and denomination.

7. Learn the early warning signals of potential malfeasance and appropriate intervention techniques.

8. Foster healing and growth beyond damage control. This includes designing more careful hiring procedures, establishing adequate accountability by all church leaders, developing policies and skills for intervention where malfeasance is occurring, and strategizing about the legal liabilities that often inhibit confession, testimony, and forgiveness.

One of the great losses resulting from the years of denial and coverup of clergy malfeasance by the church is the loss of our integrity with confession and forgiveness. Clergy, denominational executives, and parishioners have often been willing to trade spiritual integrity and justice for what seemed discreet and comfortable silence. When the secular courts and legislatures became more willing to criminalize clergy malfeasance, the financial and career penalties suddenly became too high for many to risk confession or even legal testimony. Who can expect victims (primary or secondary) to forgive when the focus is on compensation through lawsuits? It is not adequate for church leaders and theologians to urge confession, forgiveness, and integrity without providing realistic support for those they expect to take the risks and pay the penalties in clergy malfeasance. We now know that ethics (of any kind) has a price tag. This is the reason we cannot afford triumphalism when a perpetrator is caught. This is the reason that clergy support systems, though costly, are a bargain compared to increasing lawsuits. This is also the reason that the church needs to understand and commit money to education of clergy, laity, and denominational executives regarding malfeasance, prevention, and excellence in spiritual leadership.

The process of intervention also needs considerable study and use, especially in denominations without a strong central hierarchy empowered to act in clergy placement. When we speak of intervention in clergy malfeasance today, we are usually referring to the addiction model rather than the church jurisdiction model. In the addiction model, the offender is surrounded by a group of persons powerful enough to stop the offending behavior, remove the offender from the situation, and mandate appropriate treatment and recovery. Such a group usually includes a trusted friend or family member, a denominational/congregational executive, and a treatment professional. There are legal ramifications to all this, so it needs to be managed wisely. The church is learning that the risks of interventions are now less risky and are more honorable than trying to sustain the status quo.

PREVENTION GUIDELINES

Church leaders need to consider the short- and long-term prevention process. Without sensitive policies and good judgment, the church may succumb to reactive behavior in the face of the rising incidence of scandal. The situation calls for sensitive insights and proactive strategies.

The media move us to focusing on victims and the approximately 10 percent of clergy who have transgressed. These obviously need our attention, but this is short-term strategy. After completing the first six steps in the scandal management guidelines listed above, we can take on the development of long-term prevention and growth. With wise planning, more of our attention and resources can be devoted to developing procedures that move the spiritual leaders of the church (clergy and laity) toward excellence in ministry. In such planning we need to take note of two groups: the 15 percent of clergy on the verge of malfeasance (beyond the 10 percent of those already committing malfeasance); and the 75 percent of clergy who are functioning well without malfeasance but who are becoming more vulnerable as societal pressure on the clergy role increases.

Specific guidelines for prevention are becoming clear from our research. They are presented in an acronym to focus, organize, and make them more memorable. The acronym is PREVENT.

P The *P* in our acronym stands for *preparation*. Intimate and vulnerable situations will occur. Preparing for them ahead of time is one of our most valuable preventatives. As clergy we have a responsibility to help people in their times of need. We also have a responsibility to set appropriate limits on our assistance. This is done best with advance planning.

One important preventative, for instance, is establishing guidelines for physical contact between clergy and their parishioners (or even between clergy). In many churches, from charismatic to liberal, the passing of the peace, hugging, and touching are common. How can such seemingly loving and spiritual gestures be wrong? Problems and confusion arise because of mental disorders (parishioners incapable of understanding legitimate expressions of love), nefarious intent (clergy or parishioners seducing or testing each other), affection deficits (one or both parties in need of more affection), and undue familiarity (when coworkers allow themselves too many physical and emotional liberties). The laying on of hands in healing situations, the brief salutatory or spiritual embrace in public, and the caring touch by a pastor (on head, shoulders, arms, or hands only) will usually be welcome and helpful. But pastors should be alert to misinterpretation (by others and by themselves) and should ask permission or discuss such touching when in doubt. Denominations, congregations, and clergy groups need to spend time discussing and establishing policy on these matters.

R   The second letter stands for *regularity*. This means a consistent pattern for pastoral care. People think they know what a clergyperson will do in helping a needy parishioner. But they really do not know. This makes them vulnerable to the power of our office and charisma. We, too, may not always know what to do in a particular situation. By remembering our training and our mission under God, we can be confident. By consulting with other clergy and professional peers, we can be systematic without being rigid.

When I am asked to testify at court trials of clergy and pastoral counselors, the key question is, Was this clergyperson's behavior commonly accepted practice? In other words, would another normally competent clergyperson have behaved in the same way? Our guideline then is "normally accepted practice," or, in the light of the lawsuits now occurring, how will this behavior sound when reported in a courtroom?

E   The third letter is the first of two *E*s. This one stands for *evaluation*. We use this word to remind ourselves of the value of accountability and periodic review. Contrary to our common feeling that we have too many bosses in the congregation, it is likely that there is little actual accountability for our behavior in specific circumstances. Establishing appropriate ways to be accountable to official leaders in the congregation and denomination is another valuable tool for prevention. An annual review of our professional conduct and the policies under which we minister is also useful. This can be done with a competent professional counselor or consultant.

V   This letter stands for *value* and reminds us of the importance of our personal needs. This means taking our needs for intimacy very seriously. By intimacy I mean consistent, two-way, emotional closeness by agreement. Like any normal person, clergy need someone to pay attention to them, to love them, and to care for them. These needs are so important that they will be met if not in appropriate relationships, then through inappropriate ones. We can ill afford to be negligent of our marriages, family ties, and close friendships. Since spirituality is the core of our calling, our need for closeness to God also needs to be emphasized.

E   This stands for *excellence*. This is not a gratuitous scolding for laziness; it is a reminder of the joy of ministry. Few goals are more satisfying and productive than growing to be the best that we can be with help from God and our friends.

N   The N stands for *network*. This is a strong suggestion that we associate regularly with our peers—peers in ministry and in other professions. One of the clearest danger signals for clergy is when they become loners. It is an antidote and asset to be associated with other respected leaders in the community.

T   The last letter, *T*, stands for *terror*—the powerful emotion we call fear. I urge this dynamic somewhat facetiously and guardedly. We all know that ministry based upon fear will be limited and stressful. But I am serious about reminding ourselves of the terrible consequences of moral malfeasance—for ourselves, those close to us, and for pastoral ministry.

We should be aware of treatment issues when we plan for prevention. The prevention guidelines presented above will not be adequate for clergy suffering from mental disorders and addictive disabilities. Such clergy require special assistance. The church needs to become more sophisticated quickly about mental disorders and personality types that do not fit typical pastoral expectations. Psychological testing of candidates for ministry and practicing clergy has been helpful. But multiple tests and highly skilled professionals are necessary before such testing becomes reliable and instructive. Along with testing, the church needs clear and enforced codes of ethics to guide the undisciplined or overdisciplined personality types. It needs a method of assessment whereby early warning signals are taken seriously and reliable intervention, treatment, and furlough or career exit counseling are provided. There are identifiable early warning signals that should be checked when seen in a pastor, especially if these characteristics appear in clusters: excessive privacy, addictive behavior patterns, rigid-pietistic attitudes, brooding, denial of personal responsibility in problems, aloofness, compulsive socializing, compulsive touching, careless management of money, inappropriate spending, increasing criticalness, regular association with one person (not spouse), inattention to spouse and family, one-track life-style (has no apparent interests outside of pastoring), overwork. These are not indicators of sexual malfeasance in themselves, but in the lives of malfeasors these appear in clusters.

The counseling, treatment, and rehabilitation received by malfeasors need careful attention also. Sexual offenders are not understood or handled well in some psychotherapeutic settings, especially when they are clergy. Some kinds of mental and sexual disorders are not curable, only manageable, with present resources. It is no longer excusable for sexual offenders with serious disorders to be passed from one religious jurisdiction to another, or be returned to their former setting and status without appropriate supervision.

BEYOND PREVENTION

The discussion of guidelines for managing and preventing the scandals of clergy sexual malfeasance prepares us for considering larger dimensions of prevention, namely, the establishing of systemic strategies for clergy development toward excellence, and for the support of clergy in their lives and ministries.

It should be apparent by now that the role of clergy is no longer clear, to clergy, parishioners, denominational executives, seminaries, or the general public. But for the present and for the immediate future, excellence in pastoring will consist of faithful performance of the traditional functions, along with occasional opportunities for prophetic creativity. What appears to be normal, traditional functioning by clergy masks the significant changes. Clergy are expected to handle more complex situations. They must compete for attention with the media. There are fewer volunteers. There is less respect for the clergy role. More single and women clergy feel unsupported by a system designed to support male, married, caucasian pastors. The statistics of trouble are increasing as we see more divorce, burnout, addiction, malfeasance, and resignations among clergy. We are learning that higher salaries and quick-fix programs are inadequate to support pastoral ministry. We need revisions in the way we think of clergy support, and we need new ingredients for support. In short, we need a systemic change in clergy support if we are to prevent crises and sustain the average clergyperson for faithful ministry.

Having noted the need for an overhaul of clergy support *systems*, we now need to focus on the support *principles* that help prevent moral malfeasance and encourage excellence.

Principle 1. The health of the clergy is crucial to the health of the church. We cannot expect moral integrity and inspiring spiritual leadership from clergy who are exhausted, confused, and unappreciated. Therefore, appropriate systemic support is a priority.

Principle 2. Everyone needs a pastor in the generic sense. Pastors are providing this function for others while typically doing without a pastor themselves. Denominational executives, family, and close friends try to help but may end up burdening the load rather than lightening it. Pastors must be encouraged to become their own pastor, that is, they must take their own normal needs seriously and provide for them. Without such nurture, the consequences are predictable.

Principle 3. The church must provide clergy with the raw ingredients for nurture and support as the pastor utilizes them. Some of the ingredients are familiar, and some are relatively new. Pastors should have access to adequate income, insurance, pension, continuing education, sabbaticals, and equipment for pastoral functioning. But they need strong denominational support as they do what is necessary to nurture themselves and their families. Such support is absent when the pastor knows that if he displeases a congregational power broker, even while taking care of himself appropriately, he will have to move.

Principle 4. Beyond resources and support for using them in self-nurture, we now know that sometimes in their careers clergy need professional counseling, not because they are weak, but because the task is complex. When clergy are forced (or choose) to go it alone, they are likely to make the same mistakes as anyone else. Such mistakes are costly when made by a person whom many people depend upon for guidance and support. Businesses and other professions realize this. The church makes a grave mistake if it does not provide for and support clergy when they need professional counseling.

Principle 5. Peer support groups are now a necessity in the profession. This is not the traditional ministerium and "old boy network." We are seeing the value of consistent membership and participation in professional groups that affirm, critique, and guide members. This adds a balance to all the groups where the pastor is expected to be the supporter, guide, and liturgist.

Principle 6. The church is just beginning to realize that it can no longer assume that everyone understands its codes of ethics. Considerable attention must be given to upgrading, interpreting, and disseminating ethical codes for spiritual leaders in the church.

Principle 7. The wealth of writings and teachings on spirituality remind us of the importance of this dimension of human experience. Clergy are not likely to minister to human yearnings for spirituality unless they are reminded that this is their primary ministry and then encouraged and supported as they maintain their own spiritual disciplines.

In this book we have identified, defined, and discussed a serious problem in the church—clergy sexual malfeasance. What we are seeing in the media and pastoral counseling offices is only the tip of the iceberg. The scandal of moral malfeasance by church leaders must be addressed seriously from within the church in order to balance the wave of mistrust, panic, judgmentalism, and voyeurism initiated by publicized clergy malfeasance. We have resources and grace adequate to correct this unacceptable phenomenon. Beyond this attention to clergy moral malfeasance, the church is moving, often unwittingly, toward a social condition that will require pastoral ecology. Such pastoring will require exceptional sensitivity, creativity, and discernment on the part of religious leaders. We must clear the decks of the distractions of clergy malfeasance if we are going to guide humanity toward the purposes of God in creation.

17

CELIBACY AND NOUVELLE SEX

Several chapters in this book concentrate on specific unhealthy sexual practices and on problematic sexual issues. We need to balance our perspective by discussing the goodness, pleasure, joy, and creative options of human sexuality and appropriate sexual activities.

CELIBACY

Celibacy is, to common sense, an unusual management of sexuality and energy. Sexual intercourse is regarded as normal; abstinence often is assumed to be abnormal. Yet millions of human beings have lived and are living in total or periodic celibacy, without detrimental consequences. For some, in fact, it is the answer to boredom, sexual oppression, sexually transmitted diseases, and the desire to use energy in other ways.

Traditional Perspectives

Celibacy in its traditional form is associated by most persons with the Roman Catholic priesthood and religious life. In the form most known to us, religiously vowed celibacy was conceived not only as good but as part of the highest devotion to God. It was regarded primarily not as deprivation or abstinence but as the way to reserve one's total person, energy, and attention for service to God and humankind. It was also understood as a vowed expression of devotion and obedience by men and women (priests, brothers, sisters) who wished to live apart from earthly passions and distractions.

On the negative side, Christian views of sexuality grew out of a philosophy that viewed the human body as less good and worthy than the human mind and soul. In fact, the Hellenistic influence on Christian theology regarded the body as an unclean or subversive influence on the soul. All sorts of restrictions and even masochistic practices, therefore, were established to avoid the soul's enslavement and contamination by the body and to facilitate holiness.

One of the oppressive effects of this perspective was the idea of woman as seductress, as the primary source of man's distraction and immorality. The association of holy men and holy women in religious orders was carefully restricted. Furthermore, as women were regarded as sources of immorality, men, by implication, were presumed to be more rational and more worthy of authority. The hierarchical notion of men in command and women in support roles was thus reinforced.

A further largely negative consequence of this view is the idea that religious professionals should be set apart (vowed and ordained) from laypersons and thus be superior in spiritual matters. This set-apartness was influential until the Renaissance in Western civilization's view of the spiritual realm as superior to the mundane. Even when the church was no longer regarded as the absolute measure of all things, clergy and religious were regarded as different from ordinary citizens in holiness, worth, and right to respect. Ordination still tends to isolate clergy from laity, resulting in misunderstandings and encouraging the power struggles so common to congregations and within denominations.

Spirituality Versus Sexuality

This perspective has had a lasting effect on Western civilization's view of human sexuality. Sexual expression was regarded as a sign of weakness, human sexuality as separate from spirituality. The current sexual and gender revolution is in large part a rebellion against stultifying religion, and there is now some evidence that this revolution may precipitate the reunion of sexuality and spirituality in human thinking and behavior. Evidence of resistance to this reunion can be seen in the struggle over the ordination and advancement of women, the insistence on retaining celibacy for priests in the Roman Catholic Church, and in the judgmental denunciation of homosexuality, some sexual practices, contraceptives, and choice in regard to abortion.

Corollary to these hierarchical struggles in the church is an emerging awareness that there are at least two versions of spirituality in the Bible, not just one. Redemptionist theologies, which begin with creation and Fall and stress conversion and prescriptive behavior as the way to salvation, remain dominant (Billy Graham is still the most recognized proponent); but there are contemporary theologies based on human goodness (the work of Matthew Fox is probably the best known of these), in which incarnation becomes the focus, and the promotion of justice, healing, and love defines the work of salvation.

Strategic Abstinence

It is difficult to separate the idea and practice of celibacy from the negative stereotypes and symbolic traditions that seem so unnatural and unattractive. Yet strategic abstinence from sexual involvements offers real benefits as a way of life for some, as temporary respite from sexual stimulation for others, and as an opportunity to focus energies on urgent or intense missions for still others. These reasons may be combined, of course. The point is that human beings do not need typical sexual activities in order to be healthy. Furthermore, the sublimation of sexual passion and energy into valuable tasks and missions in life is not only possible but often desirable.

A key to the positive experience of strategic abstinence as energy management lies in its being voluntary. When it is imposed by authority, there will inevitably be a reactive response from all but dependent personalities. Vows, worthwhile alternatives such as nouvelle sex, and nobility of intent do not eliminate sexual curiosity and desire, even as fasting does not eliminate hunger and the need for nourishment. But voluntary practice allows one to function within one's own integrity and self-management skills, with the aid of God's grace and support by the community of faith.

Strategic abstinence need not interfere with or even limit intimacy in primary relationships. We all know that we can love our children, our parents, and close friends without engaging in sexual intercourse or sexual flirtations with them. The same is true of relationships with a spouse. All the activities and expressions of affection, respect, and collaboration can be sustained, and perhaps enhanced, with the practice of abstinence, when there is agreement about it. With clergy couples whose sexual intimacy has degenerated into a power struggle, this form of celibacy is sometimes suggested as part of the prescription for restoration of trust and affection.

In order to avoid panic reactions, conscious and unconscious, strategic abstinence needs to be considered thoughtfully—as a positive alternative, not as a remedy or discipline. Sexual needs are part of being human, and our society has an assumed entitlement regarding sexual expression that reaches deep into our unconscious selves. An act of will seldom abrogates these factors. But a temporary or modified abstinence can be effective, especially if it is supported by an intimate collaborator and satisfying life-styles.

When a pastor or clergy couple decides for some reason to explore abstinence, I encourage a careful decision process and perhaps some trial periods. If it is chosen, it needs to be supported by adequate motivation, spiritual disciplines (positive, not negative), healthy activities, and adequate attention to personal affection, sensual satisfaction, and realistic pacing of schedule and energies. Loneliness, tension, and exhaustion make intentional abstinence difficult. When strategic abstinence is a personal decision, the individual retains personal responsibility for managing it effectively (including the issue of masturbation). When it is done within a primary intimate relationship, each party experiences consequences. Therefore, there is a shared responsibility for management, especially when it is used to break an unwholesome sexual pattern within primary relationships.

Masturbation

The issue of strategic abstinence requires that some attention be given to masturbation. Masturbation is certainly not automatically included with strategic abstinence. Traditional theology and institutional practice of celibacy in fact frown on or forbid self-sex. By definition, pure celibacy excludes physical orgasm, except spontaneous ones. But in practice celibacy has taken a variety of forms, including masturbation to orgasm as the alternative to sexual intercourse. It is appropriate at times when one's partner has agreed not to be available. It is inappropriate when preparation for the act involves one in pornography or when one feels guilt after the act. A better method of strategic abstinence is to sublimate sexual passion on other activities.

NOUVELLE SEX

A phenomenon of our day is voluntary sexual enhancement either as a replacement for orgasm or as the main objective, with orgasm as a possible byproduct. Sometimes this is a response to boredom, to confusion, or to fear; but often it is a positive effort to bring sexuality back into a wholesome perspective and life-style. Nouvelle sex (also called enhanced sensuality, sex without sex, and noncoital sex) is not generically new, of course. It has been a life-style of some throughout history. The new sex is the practice of enhancing shared sensual experience without focusing on intercourse.

For those who regard sexual intercourse and orgasm as the ultimate sexual experience and the goal of sexual encounters, a primary reeducation and practice must take place before noncoital sex can be appreciated. There must be a shift from focusing on immediate gratification to savoring the extended, passionate process of shared sensual experience. The alternative pleasure of sensuality and deferred gratification requires the conscious, rational management of a natural and powerful human need. It is learned behavior, accomplished not by intention only but by accepting the rationale for it, trying it, practicing it, savoring it, and refining it. These are the same five steps used to establish rational management of nearly any appetite or feeling.

There are various versions of nouvelle sex, but all must be agreed to by both or all partners. Some partners agree never to have sexual intercourse but to stimulate passion in any ways acceptable to both. Some partners concentrate on stimulation of sight, sound, taste, smell, or touch. Some partners, usually close friends, let their attraction to each other and their sexual energy be expressed by exchanging compliments, gifts, conversation, shared activities, and attention to each other's unique characteristics. Still others devote themselves to passionate tasks or crusades and express their sexual energies by working side by side. Nouvelle sex even seems to satisfy the yearning of some people for spiritual communion.

Spirituality and Sensuality

This spiritual dimension would seem to make nouvelle sex a natural experience for the church to promulgate. But the church is typically too concerned about propriety, theological rules, and fear of the nontraditional to encourage it. The inordinate fear of sexuality and loss of decorum or control makes even the discussion of noncoital sex anathema. This is unfortunate, for noncoital sex can be an acceptable alternative to intercourse and pregnancy, and to frigidity of the emotions.

The de-emphasis or limitation of genital intercourse fits increasing attention to the spiritual dimensions of life very well. It shifts attention and energy from genital gratification and manipulation of others for our pleasure to relationship, joy, and service. With attention and energy available to invest in love of God and service to others, there can be deeply satisfying growth in spiritual awareness, discernment, and passion. The ecstasy and joy of being in love with God is an experience worth seeking because it is the full-circle union of the Creator's love for creation experienced and reciprocated at an awesome level.

Do sensuality and spirituality really go together? Strange as it may seem, here is a question on which charismatics, fundamentalists, evangelicals, conservatives, liberals, radicals, Catholics, Protestants, Jews, Muslims, Buddhists, and Hindus can agree—whether they know it or not. Spirituality can be sensual, and sensuality can be spiritual. In fact, they are mutually enhancing. The hand clapping, singing, praying, and visioning so common to religions can stimulate feelings of various kinds. The newer, nonpietistic definitions of spirituality presume an emotional or experiential component. The experience of surrender and letting go are part of spirituality. The experience of becoming one with God and with other believers is intimate and sexual in noncoital ways. The peace, ecstasy, and mind expansion of spirituality may also be understood in sexual-sensual as well as spiritual perspectives.

Nouvelle sex has the potential to bring together more people than either open or free sex or total abstinence. Nearly all persons can congregate voluntarily and with some kind of pleasure around sensual experiences—witness community celebrations, shared meals, theater, ceremonial fires, and wine tasting. The blending of spirituality, sensuality, and community is a reminder of the legitimacy of enhanced feelings and sensuality.

There remains, however, an exciting and private dimension of intimacy in nouvelle sex for partners who wish to stimulate, enhance, savor, and share the passion of fragrances, music, food, and so forth with the conscious intent to raise each other's sense experience to ecstatic levels—as an end in itself. It is little wonder that sex becomes a battleground for many couples when sexual intercourse is expected to be the totality of intimacy. Intercourse is unable to bear this level of expectation, particularly when men, as the stereotype portrays it, tend to see sex as the path to pleasure and women tend to see it as the path to

love and security. But enhanced sensuality shared with compatible or accepting partners has almost limitless ability to
nurture intimacy.

Barriers to Nouvelle Sex

I have found that there are three typical reasons why clergy
couples do not engage in this satisfying "sex without sex" process:
gender programming, habit, and time and energy.

Gender programming restricts shared enjoyment of enhanced
sensual experiences as an alternative to sex because women and
men tend not to trust each other. Without deep trust it is nearly
impossible to surrender rational control of passionate experience.
As long as the senses are inhibited rationally, there will be no
ecstasy. Perspective, socialization, biochemistry, roles, and physical sensations are different for men and women; while these differences can be exciting, they are more typically barriers. We
have to teach each other to trust us in sensual intimacy because
the trusting is what is difficult, especially when each fears that
the other will want coitus or when the persons have different
approaches to reality. The mechanics are relatively simple. We
should note here that what appear to be gender differences or
gender programming can also be personality characteristics. The
spontaneous, artistic, playful personality, and the methodical,
rational personality may well have trouble finding compatible
experiences of enhancement together.

Habits dominate our lives when no one questions them, be-
lieves they can be changed, knows how to change, or is willing
to change. The practices established in dating and early marriage tend to become life-styles, and life-styles tend to become
permanent characteristics. Competing, bickering, and hurting
each other over sexual intimacy tend to become so habitual that
the use of the senses to broaden, nurture, and enhance sexual
intimacy is no longer conceivable without outside assistance.

The lack of time and energy tends to sabotage the possibility
of nouvelle sex. The time of day and the urgency of other energy-
consuming tasks, circadian rhythms and the amount of energy

they make available, and each individual's sense of timing tend to be limiting factors. Sensual enhancement requires anticipation, initiation, stimulation, and shared savoring of the experience. All of the stages require time and energy, but together they can produce satisfying and energy-increasing experiences.

It should be obvious that nouvelle sex can be monosex. In fact, some personality styles and life situations make solo intimacy the only or preferred option. When the sensual enhancement is shared, there is an added dimension, for there are two perspectives, two energy systems, and two memory tracks. But solo sensuality has most of the same possibilities as shared sensuality, except that your partner is yourself. If you are your own best friend, and have good self-esteem, nouvelle sex can be a satisfying way to pace your life, give yourself love gifts, and savor past or distant relationships. Again, the goal is sensual pleasure, not orgasm, although orgasm can be part of the process. The danger is narcissism.

There are manuals, articles, books, and tapes available now to assist with understanding and producing the sensual enhancement of nouvelle sex. But simply learning it together, without outside resources, or even by yourself, is an experience worth the effort.

We have taken time to discuss sensual enhancement positively because it is a relatively new phenomenon that many religious people might fear. Sensual enhancement, like any gift from God, can be abused. From the glue-sniffers to the overeaters to those who become abusive without constraint, sensual stimulation clearly has its perils. Self-awareness and self-management skills are crucial if sensual enhancement is pursued. It should not be indulged in the absence of self- or group control.

18

INTIMACY

Intimacy is an art, not a science. It is built upon physical-emotional-spiritual experience rather than mechanistic data. There is no magical formula for producing intimacy, only artistic efforts. This chapter contains some guidelines for those who choose to use them.

A DEFINITION OF INTIMACY

In my working definition, human intimacy is consistent, two-way emotional closeness by agreement.

Consistency, in this definition, is important because human passions ebb and flow. Without intentional investments in the relationship, on a regular basis, we are limited to mercurial episodes of intimacy. In other words, we need to discipline ourselves to feed a relationship, even when we do not feel like it, because this can nourish the closeness we each need.

Two-way closeness is important, lest one partner become the giver and the other the taker. It is workable for one partner to take the lead in some areas of intimacy, while the other initiates other areas. But typical stereotypes and gender limitations can be avoided if leadership is periodically exchanged in intimacy.

Emotions are significant because they are the primary ingredients of our experience. Physical sensations, thoughts, and spiritual affinity are important, of course, but my experience indicates that emotional bonding between persons is the core of intimacy. This is one of the reasons males in our culture typically have more difficulty with intimacy than females. We have been programmed to de-emphasize feelings and emphasize rationality, to forgo bonding and settle for occasional encounters.

Closeness is the concept we attach most readily to intimacy. Each person has a fantasy life and sustains the emotional experience of closeness with touchable symbols invested with shared feelings (photographs, rings, a favorite song, and so forth). Being able to see, touch, and experience each other's presence is what intimacy is all about. This, of course, requires us to see and experience the other person as he or she really is—both defects and assets. Without this unconditional acceptance and appreciation, we are married to a fantasy rather than to a real person. We need to note here that in our erotically saturated society, closeness usually means sex, especially to men. In my definition, intimacy may include sex but is not limited to or defined by sexual intercourse.

Agreement is both an old and a new ingredient in intimacy. It has always been necessary to have agreements if two or more people were to live together in safety. But in human history, such close relationships as marriage, family, and friendships were almost always based upon gender and social roles. Women performed one set of roles and men another. The only task was to do one's part as well as possible and to cooperate. Now we have applied the ideal of equality to closeness. We believe we can conceptualize it, but producing it together in the relationship on which we depend for affection and support requires intentional, shared effort. None of us can impose our personal definition of equality on another person—not if we want intimacy.

AGENDAS FOR HUMAN BEHAVIOR

My experience indicates that there are three versions of intimacy. This is because humans perceive themselves in three ways, have three styles of behavior, three basic needs, and three ways of presenting themselves to the world. I call these the three agendas; the deep human realities they deal with are survival, identity, and relationship. Each of these agendas is organized around an identifying motivation, so strong that it overrules any other. Stimuli and suggestions not compatible with this motivation are screened out; any conversation, experience, or idea that does not fit the dominating agenda does not exist in the person's consciousness.

Survival Agenda

The identifying motivation is to answer the question, Is it safe here—how will I survive? The identifying law is the "law of the jungle." The identifying emotions are fear and pleasure (polarity).

Persons on this agenda tend to think in either/or terms and to resist change, unless it offers an obvious aid to their survival and pleasure. Extroverted types will be belligerent or defensive. Introverted types will be quiet and stubborn. Survivors relate readily to those they perceive as allies and resist persons they perceive as enemies. They will attack or resist with ferocity and tenacity, as jungle animals do with enemies. Their lives will be organized around protective rituals (fear). Their coping mechanisms or stress reducers will focus on comforting, sensual materials and activities (pleasure). They tend to interpret communication with others in terms of threats or reassurance. If they perceive assurance of safety, they can move to a higher agenda.

The behavior of persons who choose to function on the survival agenda will exhibit the effects of fear and pleasure seeking—the most powerful of human emotions. Neither of the other agendas can match the emotional power of this one. This agenda is triggered whenever there is disruption, significant (to the individual) change, or some strong precipitating experience (flashbacks, injuries, crises). Persons on this agenda respond readily to other persons on this agenda, if this does not pose a threat. Behavior may be crude and obvious, or sophisticated and subtle.

AGENDAS FOR HUMAN BEHAVIOR

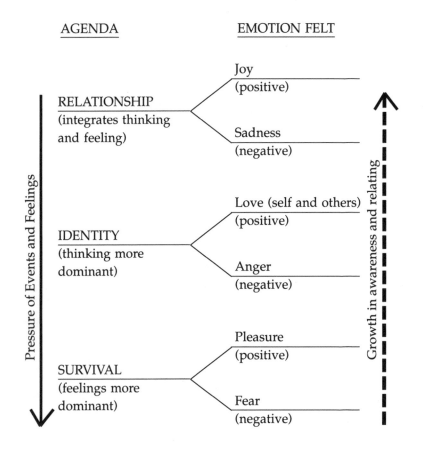

Many nice, normal people never get beyond this agenda in their lives. Many mentally disordered persons are limited to the gross or violent versions. Reassurance, then, is critical to the positive management of this agenda.

Since the basic needs of this agenda are safety, nurture, freedom, and pleasure, intimacy at this level means a relationship that meets these needs in some way. Arguing or trying to change a survivor's mind will be fruitless. But offering reassuring materials and rituals can modify behavior. Acceptable activities (private or shared) will feature physical activity, expressions of bravado, sensual pleasures, nest building, and rituals celebrating security. When these reassurances are indulged adequately, survivors are ready to consider higher agendas, if they or their partners know how to trigger the identifying factors of the desired agenda.

Identity Agenda

The identifying motivation is to answer the question, Who am I—what difference do I make? The identifying law is the "law of competition." The identifying emotions are anger and love (polarity).

The characteristics of this agenda are similar to those of survival. But this agenda is less predatory and more socialized. Persons on this agenda are highly sensitive to their own personhood. Consciously or unconsciously, they struggle with the question, What's in it for me?

Persons on this agenda tend to think in terms of life as a stage drama with themselves as the central character. They compare themselves to others if they are introverted types, and compare others to themselves if extroverted. Introverts will quietly watch the drama to learn and evaluate their part. Extroverts will try to shape the drama for their own benefit. Both types will be assessing the effect of their presence. Identifiers will relate readily to others on the basis of competition, either aggressive or gentle, if they are outgoing. They will have a rich fantasy life centered around themselves, some of which may be acted out, if they are inward types. Their lives will be organized around headlines, anniversaries featuring their life-shaping events, public pronouncements, or pity parties, resentful conversation, and punishing retributions. Their stress reducers will focus on self-indulgences, affirmation from others, and self-discoveries. This is the agenda in which insight—the ability to see and understand ourselves—is most likely to develop. The self-centeredness of this agenda can be both positive and negative. Individuals concentrating on themselves may come to understand themselves at a deep level. They may become aware of the difference they can make in relationships and society. They may even develop their insight to the level of understanding the consequences of their behavior, on others as well as themselves. It is especially helpful to have a mentor on this agenda, to help shape, model, and assess the developing personality.

The needs of a person on the identity agenda are for attention, affirmation, modeling, affection, and achievement. Their primary intimate relationships, therefore, will focus on the meeting of these needs. They will be attracted, on the one hand, to persons who respond positively toward them. They will be irritated, angry, or even punishing, on the other hand, with persons who do not give them attention or affirmation. Those who give them positive regard may be rewarded by such a person's admiration, generosity, and gestures of appreciation.

The energy generated by the interaction of anger and love on this agenda can be confusing to partners and observers. Anger is avoided by most people; love is sought. Therefore one version of this agenda is appreciated and the other is not. Anger, being undesirable, may be camouflaged and repressed. Love, being appreciated, is prominent, whether sincere or contrived. We should note that love is a learned emotion. Human beings are not born with it, as they are born with built-in fear, pleasure seeking, and anger. We are born with the potential for love. But this may be shaped into distortions and misconceptions such as aggression, conflict, abuse, and manipulation. With poor models, these can be mistaken for love. This is one reason why training and positive experiences of love are so important for children. Adult intimate partners who have not learned love may be unable to express positive love, even when they wish to. Poorly socialized lovers may even mistake distorted and self-serving expressions for positive love. We also need to remind ourselves that love is not experienced as love, no matter how sincere the intention of the giver, unless it is given in ways that are perceived as love by the receiver. Hence, we often have one or both partners in an intimate relationship feeling unloved some of the time. The love gifts and interaction experienced as love by the giver have not been so experienced by the recipient. When a person's self-esteem is violated or abused (by their own behavior or by a partner), a person will likely be pushed down to the survival agenda again. Although the experiences of attention, affirmation, affection, modeling, and achievement make it possible for a person to move up to the highest of all the agendas, this will occur only when the person or a partner can trigger the motivating factors of the relationship agenda.

Relationship Agenda

The identifying motivation is to answer the question, How can we relate positively—to each other, to others, and to all of creation? The identifying law is the "law of buoyancy" (the partner will not let the other sink). The identifying emotions are sadness and joy (polarity).

This is the noblest and most tenuous of the agendas. Self-interest, disruptions, and the social milieu tend to push persons down to the survival agenda with enormous pressure. A counterneed to relate and to generate positive consequences for the survival of the species pushes upward, but with much less perceived urgency. The dynamics of this agenda concentrate on common concerns and sharing, while the others tend to be individualistic. However, the energy generated by the polarity of the emotions identifying this agenda are similar to the others.

Persons on this agenda tend to be aware of the needs and agendas of other persons—those immediately within their partnerships and groups as well as outsiders. Extroverts on this agenda will solicit feelings and needs and express their own. Introverts are patient and supportive. Both have an expanded consciousness of human feelings, behavior, shared consequences, human limits, and a sense of the holy.

It is significant to note that anxiety and distress are lessened on this agenda. The frightening survival questions and the anxiety-producing identity questions are being answered. Life does not have to be managed alone. One may relax and float or swim because the partnership or group will not let members sink. With this lessening of distress and anxiety, coping mechanisms and stress reducers are needed less. Therefore, there is energy available for caring and ministries. Individual gifts and graces become apparent and useful for all participants. Persons on this agenda do not ignore their own needs; they have learned to meet them modestly. It is natural and satisfying for them to seek to be helpful to others and to fulfill their responsibility in creation.

Individuals, couples, and families on this agenda do not suddenly find life easy and relationships compatible. But they waste less energy and resources on counterproductive and competitive activities. They learn and use synergy—the power of unified efforts. All participants contribute and all benefit.

Sadness, on the one hand, is the negative (an indication of polarity, not a judgmental term) emotion that marks this agenda. There is a profound pain in the loss of relationships, missed opportunities to share and understand human needs, and the conflict and destruction of irresponsible human behavior and thinking. This sadness promotes neither aggression (as does anger) nor flight (as does fear). It responds to human need with empathy, even though it suffers with the thought of what might have been. Joy, on the other hand, is an exquisitely delicious emotion that celebrates what is greater than itself. It relishes responsibility (within limits), sharing (in appropriate ways), and the pleasure, love, and joy of others. Joy fuels ministries, and sadness pushes people to try again, more creatively.

It is not hard to imagine what happens to primary intimate relationships when one or both partners function on the relationship agenda, even part of the time. But individual marriage partners, couples, and families who know how to answer the needs of the lower agendas and trigger the motivating factors of the higher agendas can spend much of their lives on the relational agenda. It is true that many of life's pressures push people downward to the survival level. But it is also true that people can learn how to move quickly up through the agendas to the highest level. It works best when it is not done alone.

The three agendas discussed here occur for families and groups, as well as for individuals and couples. Complications arise when relating persons are on different agendas, or changing quickly. But it is helpful to know what the agendas are.

THE MYTHS OF INTIMACY

Many of the problems and failures of intimate relationships are related to misinformation, poor models, and unexamined social traditions. Unfortunately, such myths abound; four are listed here, framed in the traditional language of husband and wife.

The first myth is that a good wife will have a happy husband, and a good husband will have a happy wife. The truth is that if both partners care deeply for each other, it is likely that they will both be happy. But this depends upon mutuality, self-management, and cooperation. The falsehood is that we are somehow responsible for our partner's feelings, have the power and the right to control them, and know what happiness is for that person. There is fallacy also in the belief that by devoting myself to another person, I will become happy. Deep satisfaction results from caring for and supporting another person. But as much harm as good is likely to be done by a person who does not first appropriately meet her or his own real needs, so that she or he will have energy and confidence to pay attention to the other person's real needs, instead of projecting his own onto her.

The second myth is that love cures all. The truth is that sincere, honest love is extremely important to intimacy. The fallacy lies in believing that love is always affection, should be oblivious to reality, and has no limits. What solves most of the problems of intimacy is the developed ability to bring out the best in each other, and negotiate differences.

The third myth is that a truly loving partner will understand me and do what I want, when I want, and how I want. The truth is that it is a primary task of intimacy to learn who your partner really is, including needs and wants. It is not true that your partner can read your mind. Furthermore, doing what you want may feel good, but it is not the definition or test of love.

The fourth myth is that God will make clergy marriages and families function well. The truth is that God's grace and the joy of ministry can enhance clergy marriages and families, but frequently the strains of role performance, long hours, poor compensation, and extensive availability to parishioners rather than to spouse and family seriously impair intimacy. Many clergy have learned that God does not relieve them of normal marital, family, and friendship responsibilities.

Awareness of these myths can serve as encouragement to examine our personal thinking about intimacy. Our expectations and assumptions often set us up for disappointments—to ourselves and to those dear to us. It is normal for each person, even the shy and the weak, to have strong beliefs about how marriage and intimate relationships should work. When these conscious or unconscious beliefs are not fulfilled, it is also natural for a person to ask why not. Passive persons then tend to blame themselves for this failure, and aggressive persons tend to blame their partners. Both then tend to store up resentments that contaminate intimacy. Wise partners know the danger of resentments and take time to express and work through them.

Our intimacy expectations and assumptions typically come from the intimate relationships we observed while growing up. They are also shaped by the formative experiences of our lives. Parents or significant adults, for example, teach us what intimacy should or should not be. We spend much of our relational

energy trying to duplicate or avoid these models. Since our partner is doing the same thing, it can help if both had the same
kinds of models, lest they work at cross-purposes, often without
realizing what is occurring. Likewise, the unknown or unacceptable parts of ourselves tend to be projected onto intimate partners, without either party realizing this.

Life-shaping events also influence our perspectives on intimacy.
I have heard clergy tell how the death of a mother at an early
age, for example, made them distrust relationships with females.
To compensate, they tend to avoid intimacy, to spread their intimacy among many women, or to expect a female partner to
become superwife—always proving love and dependability.

THE ART OF INTIMACY

We are all artists, producing the many poems and paintings,
songs, sculptures, and dramas of our lives. One of the most
important is our primary intimate relationship. By definition, this
relationship involves at least one other person, also an artist.
Thus we face the challenge of collaborating with another on joint
works. This requires the development of certain skills. Chief
among these are assertiveness, the ability to change, and the gift
of affirmation.

Our childhood programming of gender and intimacy can com-
plicate the assertiveness issue. For example, it is common for
women born before the rise of feminism not to feel they have
the right to state clearly what they want in a relationship, except
in situations in which they feel dominant or their husbands have
given them explicit permission to be assertive. Men of a similar
age typically believe that women should comply with their male
wants or beliefs. Some contemporary models of marriage still
contain such gender roles. If both agree, and no one is oppressed
by this arrangement, it can produce intimacy. But more and more
women are giving themselves permission to assert their needs
and perspectives in marriage, family, and close relationships.
More men are learning the relief of not having to dominate inti-

mate relationships and the satisfaction of having an equal partner. It does not always work out positively, of course, as the contemporary divorce rate demonstrates.

Assertiveness

Assertiveness is not aggressiveness or hostility. Assertiveness has no intention of hurting, dominating, or being self-centered. It means speaking up for what is important to you, and acting as if you believe this is worthwhile. The keys to achieving this principle are self-esteem and communication.

Self-esteem. At its center, self-esteem means believing you have value as the person you are—in religious language, that you have great value in God's sight, and thus self-worth. Cocky persons think that self-worth means they are perfect or superior persons; shy persons think it means that they ought to be. Appropriate and satisfying self-esteem is possible for both, but to gain it is not easy. A partner who becomes aware of lack of esteem should make special efforts—usually with professional assistance—to develop it. Without it, intimacy is limited.

Communication. The many ways we indicate our thoughts, feelings, and personal identity to others is communication. Words are most often used, but communication is much broader than words. Yet words are usually needed to clarify and correct our inferences from this broader sense of communication. If intimacy is a goal of relationship and if equality and freedom are important, shaping such a relationship requires intentional interaction. Words are the most efficient form of communication; but nonverbal forms (body language, behavior, and so forth) must be consistent with verbal forms to achieve clarity. Confusion usually occurs when there is no perceived consistency.

Generally speaking, most of us can use words well enough to communicate our thoughts and feelings whenever we are aware of them. So this part of communication can be relatively simple.

But memories, misconceptions, and personal agendas can give words different meanings. How we interpret what an intimate partner communicates shapes or even determines our response. If the response to communication is based upon a misinterpretation and is in turn misinterpreted, the original message or intention is quickly lost. Therefore, a critical part of communication is clarification. This requires that each partner listen and respond in ways that aid clarity.

With self-esteem and communication in a growing process, we can handle the risk of assertiveness better. It is a risk because it upsets habits and patterns in a relationship. No one can predict fully the consequences in oneself or one's partner when assertiveness is risked. Yet not risking assertiveness has consequences also—both good and bad. Assertiveness is not acceptance and passivity. It does not allow others dominance and inappropriate privilege; it is willing to speak up in the hope of improvement for all rather than accept an oppressive status quo.

Sometimes intimate partners need to learn a significant truth about communication in order to give themselves permission to be assertive: I am not responsible for negative reactions to my assertiveness—including anger, abuse, silence, and sulking. Negative reactions are the other person's responsibility. Retaining the right to define oneself and demonstrating the ability to determine one's own mood and attitude may even make it possible for a recalcitrant partner to join in healthy assertiveness.

It has been a pleasure for me to work with and to observe couples and families teaching themselves the value of assertiveness in intimacy. With practice, a person becomes adept at self-expression, as an artist becomes more skilled. The work produced, in this case an intimate relationship, can become much more satisfying.

Change

Individuals and environments change, whether or not change is wanted or recognized. When a relationship does not change, it becomes brittle or even stifling rather than supportive. Being held in it or committed to it catches the participants in a time warp.

Changing something as important as a primary intimate relationship requires courage, sensitivity, and skill. But partners in intimate relationships cannot afford to wait for perfected skills or exact timing. They need to be encouraged to trust their basic love for and commitment to each other as a foundation on which to build or rebuild their relationship. One of the most common reasons clergy couples give me for wanting to divorce is that the relationship no longer fits the needs and expectations of one or both partners.

Following the hierarchical structure of our paradigm, we consider first the survival agenda. The introduction of change to an insecure person or to someone who feels that their survival or pleasure is being threatened will meet instant resistance. So when persons or couples are interested in changing their relational patterns in some way, it is important to check the dominant emotion in their lives. If that is fear or pleasure, we know it will be safest to present the change options as contributors to safety and pleasure.

The duration of powerful emotions is relatively short. One can cater to a pleasure-seeking appetite only so long before satiation is reached. Then the pleasurable experience or item is less desirable. In fact, boredom may set in, turning what was once pleasurable into something undesirable. Fear, to a lesser degree, also is sustainable at the terror or panic level only for a limited time. All emotions are sustained by energy and a human organism's supply of it and ability to make use of it is limited to the strength of this person's system. Fear loses its intensity with time, unless the threat continues or is accelerated, in which event the human energy system is likely to collapse under the strain. Or the person may use bravado or disdain to rationalize and defuse the threat.

An illustration of the change process on the survival agenda comes from a clergy couple who represent a threat and need common to the clergy scene. This couple came to my office with a vague but strong feeling that something needed to change in their relationship. In counseling, they identified their evening pattern as the one in which both were most uncomfortable. The dinner hour was rushed. She prepared dinner. He helped a little although usually he tried to sit alone for a while to watch the news, read the paper, and drink tea or liquor. The kids were in and out. Finally the family sat down to eat. He usually ate quickly and left for some church meeting or visitation. The kids took off. She was left alone with dishes and evening prime time. Everyone returned about late TV news time, exhausted and harried. There was little interaction. Bedtime finally silenced the household.

The kids were gone now. He was beginning to feel weary of it all. She, a school teacher, was feeling bored and lonely. When they first talked about the situation, their conversation was somewhat resentful and vindictive. But the issue he kept coming back to was the urgency of his need to attend all the church meetings or make visits in the evenings. He, on the one hand, was afraid of the consequences if he did not: poor church meetings and criticism about not visiting enough. He mentioned that a seminary classmate in a church nearby was presently threatened by such conflict. She, on the other hand, kept expressing fear about what was happening to their relationship.

In the counseling process, each expressed their fears and what prompted these. Then we discussed what was important to each of them at this stage in life. We reviewed their relational history, highlighting their peak experiences and their methods of solving problems together. This moved them through the agendas and allowed us to deal with the survival agenda. Eventually he was able to go to his church board and arrange to have two evenings free each week, one fixed and one rotating according to church schedules. Together they began to explore pleasurable activities and worthwhile tasks they could do either as a couple or individually on those free nights. The change they produced in their intimacy was in large measure due to the time they took discovering the real issues and exploring realistic options.

Affirmation

Assuming normal conditions, the power of affirmation in an intimate relationship is awe inspiring. Yet to give compliments, express appreciation, and offer encouragement can be difficult. We seem to worry about sincerity, giving someone a "big head," or reciprocity. But the effectiveness of positive feedback is one of the simplest and most powerful resources for intimacy. Affirmation fits the needs and focusing questions of all three agendas for human behavior.

The elements of affirmation are attention, active listening, positive feedback, and sharing your own feelings. Paying attention to a person means making eye contact and taking time to focus on what is being shared. It is a signal of safety, affirmation, and willingness to share. Not paying attention, of course, signals the opposite. Active listening means responding to what is being communicated, without editorializing or corrections by reflecting back to the initiator what you heard or saw being communicated. Active listening gives a partner the sweet experience of having what she or he shared taken seriously and accepted at face value. Such listening is valuable also for the listener. It gives information about how the partner is experiencing what is happening, and it allows silent clarification of the listener's experience.

Positive feedback means pointedly giving signals of hearing or seeing the communication from the initiator, and acknowledging it to be true for that person. Each person has his or her own truth, that is, a personal version or experience of what is happening. It is useful to remind ourselves that the truth experienced by the other is as true for her as my truth is for me. Arguing over each other's perspective signals attack, which reduces the relationship to the survival level. Comments such as "That sounds important to you" or "I appreciate your sharing this with me" are often perceived as positive during communication. We need to note that what seems positive and affectionate to one person may not be such for a partner. To assure giving positive feedback, we need to learn each other's language of love.

Sharing your own feelings means sharing your own truth with the initiator. Ordinarily, the previous three behavior agendas allow this to be acceptable to the initiator. If she or he can respond in the same way to you, healthy dialogue occurs—even when negative feelings are shared and it is not all done perfectly.

These keys do not guarantee affectionate intimacy, but they certainly make it more likely. One of the goals of intimacy is satisfying the human need for affection and pleasure. Erotic and playful sharing on a consistent and mutually acceptable basis acts as a safeguard against inappropriate intimate relationships for either or both partners.

SELECTED BIBLIOGRAPHY

Brown, Gabrielle. *The New Celibacy.* New York: Ballantine Books, 1980.

Burgess, Ann W., and Carol R. Hartman, eds. *Sexual Exploitation of Patients by Health Professionals.* New York: Praeger Publishers, 1984.

Carnes, Patrick. *The Sexual Addiction.* Minneapolis: CompCare Publications, 1983.

Carrera, Michael. *Sex: The Facts, the Acts and Your Feelings.* New York: Crown Publishers, 1981.

Everstine, Diane Sullivan, and Louis Everstine. *Sexual Trauma in Children and Adolescents.* New York: Brunner/Mazel, 1989.

Fisher, Peter. *The Gay Mystique.* New York: Stein and Day, 1972.

Fortune, Marie M. *Is Nothing Sacred?* San Francisco: Harper and Row, 1988.

_____. *Sexual Violence.* New York: Pilgrim Press, 1983.

Gazzinga, Michael. *Mind Matters.* Boston: Houghton Mifflin, 1988.

Gilligan, Carol. *In a Different Voice.* Cambridge: Harvard University Press, 1982.

Holmes, Urban T. *Spirituality for Ministry.* San Francisco: Harper & Row, 1982.

Horton, Anne L., and Judity A. Williamson, eds. *Abuse and Religion: When Praying Isn't Enough.* Lexington, Mass.: Lexington Books, n.d.

Kaplan, Helen Singer. *The New Sex Therapy.* New York: Brunner/Mazel, 1974.

Kelsey, Morton. *Encounter with God.* Minneapolis: Bethany Fellowship, 1972.

Lebacqz, Karen. *Professional Ethics: Power and Paradox.* Nashville: Abingdon Press, 1985.

Mace, David and Vera. *What's Happening to Clergy Marriages?* Nashville: Abingdon Press, 1980.

Maloney, H. Newton, et al. *Clergy Malpractice.* Philadelphia: Westminster Press, 1986.

May, Gerald G. *Care of Mind, Care of Spirit.* San Francisco: Harper & Row, 1982.

Merrill, Dean. *Clergy Couples in Crisis.* Waco: Word Publishers, 1985.

Nelson, James B. *Between Two Gardens.* New York: Pilgrim Press, 1983.

_____. *Embodiment: An Approach to Sexuality and Christian Theology.* Minneapolis: Augsburg, 1978.

Noyce, Gaylord. *Pastoral Ethics.* Nashville: Abingdon Press, 1988.

Rediger, Lloyd. *Coping with Clergy Burnout.* Valley Forge: Judson Press, 1982.

_____. *Lord, Don't Let Me Be Bored.* Philadelphia: Westminster Press, 1986.

Rosenberg, Jean. *Fuel on the Fire.* Orwell: Safer Society Press, 1989.

Saia, Michael R. *Counseling the Homosexual.* Minneapolis: Bethany House Publishers, 1989.

Sanford, John. *The Invisible Partners.* New York: Paulist Press, 1980.

Smart, James D. *The Past, Present and Future of Biblical Theology.* Philadelphia: Westminster Press, 1979.

Swicegood, Thomas L. P. *Our God, Too.* New York: Signet, 1975.

Tripp, C. A. *The Homosexual Matrix.* New York: Signet, 1975.

Wonder, Jacquelyn, and Priscilla Donovan. *Whole Brain Thinking.* New York: Ballantine Books, 1985.